The Tramw[ays of] North Lan[cashire]

Adapted from *Great British Tramway Networks*

"The joys of Accrington lay, not in the town itself, but in the getting there. It was, of course, a tram journey. It was exhilarating to go lurching across the bare moorland, with the wires singing overhead, and the larks climbing into the sky..."

—Rachel Ryan, in *A Biography of Manchester* (Methuen, 1931).

For about two decades, up to 1930, it was possible to board an electric tram in the centre of Manchester and, with several changes of car, arrive about six hours later in Blackburn or Darwen. The section of tramway between Rochdale and Bacup was not completed until 1911, but from Bacup onwards the line was much older, having been built before 1890 by four steam tramway companies, to a gauge of 4ft 0in instead of the usual Lancashire tramway gauge of 4ft 8½in. Bacup to Whitehall (beyond Darwen), 21 miles, via Accrington and Blackburn, was the longest continuous journey possible by steam tram in Britain, and this book is designed to retrace this and other tramway journeys that once were possible in the northern part of the County Palatine.

There were in fact two separate 4ft gauge tramway networks in North Lancashire, a larger one extending from Bacup to Darwen, and a smaller one around Burnley, the two being separated by areas of moorland. Burnley Corporation possessed an extensive 4ft gauge layout, with seven routes radiating from Burnley centre, six inaugurated in 1901-12 and one, to Brunshaw, in 1927. Two of them replaced the standard-gauge steam trams which the Burnley and District Tramways Co. Ltd. had operated from 1881 from Padiham through Burnley to the centre of Nelson, seven miles, with 17 steam engines and 16 open-top cars. When Burnley Corporation electrified the company's lines, it changed the gauge to 4ft so that double track could be laid from Burnley to Nelson, and this would have allowed its tracks to be joined to those of Accrington, but the three mile gap from Rose Grove to Accrington's Cemetery terminus was never filled.

In the other direction, the Burnley tramways were connected with those of Nelson and Colne, laid to the same 4ft gauge. The steam tramway had been purchased jointly by five local authorities, so Burnley Corporation's distinctive trams (53 double-deck and 19 single-deck bogie cars) also operated on tracks owned by Nelson Corporation and by the Urban District Councils of Padiham and of Brierfield. A portion, less than half a mile, of the Burnley to Nelson route was owned by the Reedley Hallows Parish Council, the only parish council in Great Britain to have owned its own tramway.

COVER PHOTOGRAPH: Three Accrington steam trams in Peel Street in 1907, a few months before electric services began. The second car was purchased from Blackburn. Accrington, Haslingden and Rawtenstall were served by what became Britain's last urban steam tramways.

BACK COVER: A 1925 advertisement featuring Darwen tram No. 22.

Burnley, Colne and Nelson trams could be seen together at Nelson Centre. This 1919 postcard shows Nelson tram 2 on the service to Higherford, and (right) Colne tram 11 on the service to Trawden. There was probably a Burnley tram standing behind the photographer. *(Valentine & Sons, courtesy R. Brook)*

Because of a low bridge at Colne station, Burnley's trams turned back at Nelson Centre, and only very occasional special cars (open-top or single-deck) ran through to Colne. Similarly, Nelson's trams only ran to Burnley on occasional private-hire or football duties, and the sight of a Colne tram in Burnley was even rarer. Nelson Corporation's own cars, which started early in 1903, ran from Nelson centre to Higherford, and shared in a joint service from Nelson to Colne, whose tramways had been built in 1903 by the Colne and Trawden Light Railways Company, but were purchased in 1914 by Colne Corporation.

Colne also owned and operated a route to Trawden, which at two places left the main road in favour of privately-owned reserved tracks so as to follow easier gradients, and a shorter route to Laneshaw Bridge, worked latterly by two one-man single-deckers. This terminus is only nine miles from the Utley terminus of Keighley, whose tramways, like those of its neighbour Bradford, were also constructed to the same 4ft gauge. Colne had a total of 18 trams of various types, and Nelson 21.

The Colne local routes were abandoned in 1926 and 1928, Burnley closed its Harle Syke and Rose Grove routes in 1932, and the Nelson local routes ceased early in 1934. Meanwhile in 1933 all municipal transport interests in the district had been transferred to the new Burnley Colne and Nelson Joint Transport Committee, and Burnley's trams took over the working of Nelson's Barrowford route for its final months. The Joint Committee abandoned the other five Burnley tram routes, including the line to Nelson centre, in 1934-35. In 1974, Colne and Nelson were merged to form the Pendle District, and the transport undertaking was renamed Burnley & Pendle Joint Transport Committee.

Retracing our steps to Bacup, we can now start our journey over the main North Lancashire network. Rochdale Corporation trams ran to Bacup, over tracks owned by the Rochdale, Whitworth, and Bacup local authorities. In Bacup, this standard-gauge Bacup Light Railway was separated by only a short gap from the terminus of Bacup Corporation's other line, the 4ft gauge tramway to Rawtenstall purchased in 1908 from the Rossendale Valley Tramways Company, whose steam cars had run since 1889 from Rawtenstall to Bacup, and since 1891 to Crawshawbooth.

The RVTC was purchased in 1900 by the British Electric Traction Co Ltd, with a view to its electrification, but the local authorities would not agree to this, and hoped to run the lines themselves. Unfortunately, they could not agree between themselves how it was to be done, and they also had to wait until the expiry of the 21-year lease, so this rivalry kept the steam trams running until 1909, by which time the Rossendale Valley line had become Britain's last urban steam tramway. Rawtenstall Corporation then took over, with electric cars, and worked Bacup Corporation's section as an extension of its own route.

Between Bacup and Rawtenstall is Waterfoot, whence Rawtenstall built a line northwards through Lumb to Water, worked partly by single-deck cars. Rawtenstall also extended the Crawshawbooth route to Loveclough, which is only three miles distant from the Summit terminus of Burnley Corporation's steep Manchester Road route. The two were never linked, but powers were granted in 1889 and 1902. Rawtenstall's first 16 electric trams were built with regenerative control equipment, but this had to be removed from the cars after a 1910 runaway accident. By 1921 there were 32 electric trams of three different types, plus two steam tram engines kept as snowploughs, but buses replaced the trams between 1930 and 1932.

Rawtenstall municipality owned a fourth line, to Lockgate, which abutted onto the single route of Haslingden Corporation, the latter in turn connecting end-on with the Baxenden route of Accrington Corporation. The whole route had been worked until 1907-08 by the Accrington Corporation Steam Tramways Company, which also had routes from Accrington to Church and to Clayton-le-Moors, with eventually 22 engines and 20 bogie cars. This combined system opened in 1886-87, and was bought by Accrington, Haslingden and Rawtenstall Corporations in 1907. Accrington's part was soon electrified, but Haslingden Corporation ran steam trams for several months between Baxenden and Rawtenstall until this portion too was electrified, using only Accrington cars. From 1910 to 1916 Rawtenstall and Accrington worked a through joint service from Accrington to Bacup, also operating the intervening section on behalf of Haslingden. Until this ceased, four Accrington trams were kept in Haslingden's small depot, but from then on it housed only a steam tram engine and wagon used by Haslingden for track maintenance and snow clearing. An Act of 1906 authorised Haslingden to build three routes to Grane Road Cemetery, Helmshore, and Ewood Bridge, totalling 3¼ miles, but this project fell through.

Nestling in a valley between Haslingden and the Walmersley terminus of Bury Corporation is Ramsbottom, whose Urban District Council obtained powers in 1903 to construct a tramway system of 5¼ route miles. Unfortunately the work was continually postponed, though a depot was built and prominently inscribed "Ramsbottom Tramways", and in 1913 the Council became a pioneer operator of trolleybuses, only the fifth such installation anywhere in Britain, and the only such vehicles ever in North Lancashire. They ran the 3½ miles from Edenfield to Holcombe Brook until 1931, connecting there with the Lancashire & Yorkshire Railway's electric trains to Bury.

Had Ramsbottom constructed its tramways it might have provided part of another connection between the North and South Lancashire networks, though the choice of gauge would have been a problem. An earlier project was for a Turton, Tottington, Ramsbottom and Rawtenstall Light Railway, with two routes from the Tottington terminus of the Bury Tramways, one to Turton and the other via Ramsbottom and Edenfield to Rawtenstall. The parts from Tottington to Turton and to Holcombe Brook were withdrawn, and a fresh application in 1902 for a 5¼-mile line from Holcombe Brook to Rawtenstall was rejected, though granted in part to Ramsbottom UDC in 1903. Ramsbottom Council's buses were later taken over by Selnec PTE, despite having for several years shared a manager with the Rossendale Valley Transport Board, successor to the transport departments of Haslingden and Rawtenstall.

When they took over the lines of the Accrington Corporation Steam Tramways Company in 1907, Accrington Corporation not only electrified the three steam tram routes to Church, Clayton and Baxenden, but also built extensions from Church to Oswaldtwistle and also to Accrington Cemetery, with powers to continue to Huncoat. The Oswaldtwistle route passed under a low railway arch, and was worked by single-deck cars until two special low-bridge trams were bought in 1926, bringing the Accrington fleet up to 38 trams of five different types. Haslingden and Accrington abandoned their tramways in 1930 and 1932 respectively, in favour of buses, of which Haslingden owned and operated its own fleet, until it joined with Rawtenstall in 1974 to form the Rossendale Valley Transport Board.

An unfulfilled plan provided for connecting Clayton-le-Moors, and also Burnley's Padiham route, with Whalley some four miles further north. This was to have been done by the Blackburn, Whalley, and Padiham Light Railway Company, to whom fourteen miles of 4ft-gauge line were authorised in 1901. Blackburn also was to have been connected with Whalley, by way of Rishton, Great Harwood and Hindle Fold. The whole scheme was promoted by the Auxiliary and Light Railways and Tramways Co Ltd, the parent company of the BWP, and which also promoted an unbuilt Preston Chorley and Horwich tramway.

At Church, Accrington made connection with the Blackburn Corporation system, and after the withdrawal of the joint Accrington and Blackburn through service in 1931 Blackburn continued to operate a frequent tram service to Church from their side, despite the rural nature of the route and the fact that at one point there was not a building in sight. In steam tram days, starting in 1887, the Blackburn Corporation Tramways Co Ltd had leased 8½ miles of route from Blackburn Corporation, and ran 14 steam engines with 19 eight-wheel covered-top cars from Blackburn to Church, where they connected with the Accrington steam trams, and up Whalley New Road to the Cemetery. The same company ran eight open-top horse cars from Blackburn along the Preston New Road towards Billinge, and also to Witton Stocks, from 1888 to 1899, when municipal electric cars took over, Blackburn having the first overhead-wire electric tramway in North Lancashire. The steam routes were electrified in 1901. An Act of 1891 had authorised the Blackburn company (not Accrington) to build a steam tramway from Church to Oswaldtwistle.

Blackburn had an elaborate layout of one-way streets in the centre of the town, and a large amount of interlaced track, mainly on the Wilpshire route, which was a 1902 extension of that to the Cemetery. Another new route, to Audley, was

On 28th June 1900, a special steam tram took a civic party right through from Darwen's Whitehall terminus to Bacup, 21 miles. This photograph was taken at Blackburn Road, Accrington. *(TMS*

opened in 1903, and the Witton route was extended to Cherry Tree. Most of the Blackburn system flourished very efficiently until the late 1940s, and it was renowned for the exceptionally smooth riding of its large double-deck bogie cars. There were eight early open-top units, forty more of a much improved type, of which 32 were later top-covered and fitted with small wheels and motors to enable them to pass under the railway bridges, and thirteen single-deckers.

The one Blackburn route not yet mentioned ran southward to the Darwen boundary, from where the cars continued over Darwen Corporation tracks with a joint service of both authorities through the centre of Darwen to Whitehall. This five-mile line had been built in 1881 by the Blackburn and Over Darwen Tramways Company, and was the first in Britain to be authorised and operated solely by steam power, there being in due course 12 locomotives and 16 cars. It was split in two and purchased by the Corporations of Blackburn and Darwen in 1899, and electrified in 1900. In the last year of Darwen steam trams, a special car took a civic party right through from Whitehall to Bacup, taking about 4½ hours for the 21 miles.

Darwen Corporation's other route was a moorland line to Hoddlesden, climbing 250 feet in just over a mile, and worked by four-wheel cars with special brakes. Despite these, it was the scene of several serious runaways. The line to Whitehall was also quite steeply graded, and was in a direct line with the Dunscar terminus of Bolton Corporation some five miles distant, with which tramway connection by a proposed Bolton Turton and Darwen Light Railway was applied for in 1901. Darwen Corporation subsequently owned a total of 34 electric cars of six different types, including two streamlined centre-entrance cars built in 1936, which were sold ten years later to the Llandudno and Colwyn Bay Electric Railway Co Ltd. The last portions of the Darwen and Blackburn systems were replaced by motor buses in 1946 and 1949 respectively, and the two undertakings were merged as Blackburn Borough Transport in consequence of local government reorganisation in 1974.

Eight miles west of Blackburn, Preston had an isolated 10½-mile standard-gauge municipal system, opened in 1904 and replacing two separate 3ft 6in gauge privately-operated horse tramway undertakings, the 2½ miles of the Preston Tramways Company to Fulwood, and the 4¾ miles of W. Harding & Co Ltd to Ashton-on-Ribble and Farringdon Park. Electric routes extended to Penwortham Bridge, Ashton-on-Ribble, Ribbleton, and Farringdon Park, with a circular route via Fulwood. An Act of 1900 authorised 11¼ miles of new electric route and widened the gauge from 3ft 6in to 4ft 0in, whilst a further Act of 1902 increased this length to 14¾ miles and the gauge to 4ft 8½in, but only 10½ route miles of the total 14¾ were actually built. As elsewhere in North Lancashire, the existence of low railway bridges meant that there was considerable variety in Preston's tram fleet, with both four- and eight-wheeled, single- and double-deck, and open- and covered-top cars, giving a total of 48 cars plus 6 replacements, but the tramways were abandoned in 1932-35.

As recorded on page 4 of *The Tramways of South-East Lancashire*, Preston might at one time have been connected by tramway with both Bolton and Wigan, by way of Chorley, with 23 miles of electric tramway authorised in 1903 to the Preston Chorley and Horwich Tramways Company. Another company was formed in 1903 to build a 4ft gauge line from Blackburn to Preston (Farringdon Park) but this too did not materialise. There were two separate schemes for a Preston and Lytham Light Railway, which would have connected Preston's tramways with those of Lytham St Annes, but neither of them managed to get authorised, much less built.

Preston was home of the Dick, Kerr works, which built 8,350 tramcars between 1899 and 1940. This 1907 photograph shows craftsmen from Dick, Kerr's Strand Road works having just fitted a top-cover to Preston Corporation open-top tram 22, built by Dick, Kerr in 1904. *(GEC Traction Ltd.*

Preston can also claim to be the home of the tramcar, for i is on the western edge of this town that the famous English Electric Dick Kerr works are situated, now part of GEC Traction Ltd, where an estimated 8,350 tramcars were constructed over the years, culminating in the splendid streamlined double-deckers for Darwen and Blackpool in the 1930s, and similar prototype cars for Aberdeen in 1940. There was quite an extensive tramway layout inside the grounds of the works in early years, for testing newly-built cars. Dick Kerr & Co Ltd, of Kilmarnock, were already established as general engineers when in 1898 they took over a vacant factory at Preston and formed a new subsidiary, the Electric Railway & Tramway Carriage Works, Limited. In 1905 Dick Kerr purchased the British Electric Car Co Ltd of Trafford Park, Manchester, and also G. F. Milnes & Co Ltd of Hadley, Shropshire (formerly of Birkenhead), and amalgamated these two with the ER&TCW to form a new United Electric Car Co Ltd, all tramcar construction now being concentrated at the Preston Works. In 1918 the English Electric Co Ltd was formed to take over and absorb Dick Kerr, the UEC, and four engineering or electrical companies with factories at Rugby, Coventry, Stafford, and Bradford. There have been other important tramcar manufacturers at Loughborough, Motherwell, and elsewhere, whilst many large operators built at least some of their cars themselves, but far more trams were built at Preston than anywhere else in Britain.

Lytham St Annes had its own standard-gauge tramway, extending from Lytham Cottage Hospital through St Annes to Squires Gate. Originally the property of the Blackpool, St Annes and Lytham Tramways Co Ltd, it passed in 1920 to the St Annes Urban District Council, including the Lytham section, but on the amalgamation in 1922 of this council's area with that of the then-separate Lytham Urban District Council to form a new combined borough the tramway was taken over by the new Lytham St Annes Corporation. Until 1917 the Company leased 1¼ miles of tramway from Blackpool, and ran to South Shore Station. In 1917 Blackpool took over this section, reducing the Company's line from 7½ to 6¼ miles, whereupon the Lytham trams exercised running powers into Blackpool, the final terminus after several changes of route being at Gynn Square.

The Lytham tramways had an unusual history, for sixteen cars running on compressed coal gas were used from 1896-97 until electrification in 1903. The first operator was the British Gas Traction Co Ltd, and during 1901-02 the BSAL Co was owned by a short-lived Blackpool Electric Tramways (South) Ltd. The gas trams were not particularly successful, and for a time the northernmost section of line was operated with horse trams. Lytham's other terminus was intended as the start of an unusual amphibious tramway operation, for an 11-mile tramway was authorised in 1900 from Lytham St Annes to Southport, the cars to be carried across the estuary of the River Ribble by a transporter bridge, and onwards by a viaduct across the tidal sands, though the intention in 1898 had been to use a moving platform similar to that of the Brighton & Rottingdean Seashore Electric Tramroad.

A short section of Lytham-owned track formed until 1962 a strategic link at Squires Gate between two adjacent termini of the Blackpool system, but with this exception the entire Lytham system of 6¼ route miles and 56 cars was abandoned in 1936-37. In addition to conventional double and single-deck cars the Lytham fleet also contained 20 double-deck toastracks, probably the only such in the British Isles apart from Douglas Southern or the Seaton miniature line. Lytham replaced the trams with municipal motor buses, and became Fylde Borough Council in 1974, rejecting in 1982 a proposed sale of its transport to Blackpool.

At Starr Gate we can change to the present tense, for here the Lytham tracks connect with those of Blackpool Corporation, for many years the most progressive tramway in the country. The line along Blackpool Promenade, situated between the road and footwalk and neatly paved with flagstones, carries enormous holiday traffic, subject to very sudden fluctuations, which could scarcely be tackled at all by any other method. Much of it follows the line of the town's earliest tramway, a 1¾-mile conduit line of 1885 owned by the Blackpool Electric Tramway Co Ltd, which was purchased by the Corporation in 1892 and converted to the overhead-trolley system seven years later. The Promenade tramway also plays an important part in Blackpool's annual autumn Illuminations, when illuminated trams, at present representing a rocket, a hovercraft, a frigate, and a western train, run to and fro interspersed with the normal service and tour cars. There have been four other striking designs in the past.

Over the years, Blackpool gradually re-spaced its tracks to allow the operation of wider vehicles, the only British tramway operator to have done so. 141 modern centre-entrance trams were purchased from 1933 onwards, including 25 of a new 8ft-wide design introduced in 1952, and in 1960 the Corporation introduced modern centre-entrance trailers. More recently, thirteen cars have been rebuilt for one-man operation (more strictly one-person operation, for there are several lady drivers), and in 1979 a new 98-seat double-decker was built in the Corporation's workshops, where a second similar car was finished in 1982. These were joined in 1984 by a completely new single-deck car, planned to be the first of a class of ten. The present fleet consists of 26 double-deckers, plus 51 single-deckers of six different types, and ten illuminated or engineering cars. Other Blackpool tramways of the street variety formerly served Layton, the Central Drive, Squires Gate, and a Circular route via Marton. In past years there have been a further 155 cars of a dozen different types as well as the 141 modern and 41 acquired cars. Maximum route mileage (excluding Fleetwood) was 12¼.

At Gynn Square the Promenade line was joined until 1963 by the street track from the North Station, the original 1898 route of the 8¼-mile Blackpool and Fleetwood Tramroad Company, which a short distance beyond, at the Cabin, passes onto a fenced-in right of way with bullhead rails laid on sleepers. This section, purchased by Blackpool Corporation from the company in 1919, with 41 bogie single-deck cars, continues through Bispham and Cleveleys to Thornton Gate, from which point to Fleetwood the tracks were shared until 1949 by railway goods wagons to and from Thornton Gate Mineral Sidings, where some coal merchants were established. For this work Blackpool Corporation used a neat little four-wheeled electric locomotive, similar to those employed elsewhere at power stations. Entering Fleetwood the tram track regains the streets, and for its terminus it makes a loop opposite the lighthouse and ferry.

Immediately across the River Wyre from Fleetwood Ferry is Knott End, and in about 1905 the Blackpool and Fleetwood Tramroad Company proposed to purchase the Garstang and Knott End Railway, at that time not yet built between Knott End

The famous Blackpool to Fleetwood reserved-track tramway, photographed in August, 1934, with Dreadnought tram 57 passing the Miners Convalescent Home, between Cabin and Bispham. *(G. L. Gundry)*

and Pilling, and to complete this section and electrify the whole line. This proposal fell through, and the G&KER was later absorbed by the LMSR, but at a very early date the B&FTC inaugurated through bookings from Blackpool, via the tramroad and the ferry and thence by County Motors buses through to Pilling and Lancaster. These bookings as far as Pilling survived right up to the second war, long after the tramroad had been sold to the Corporation and the buses to Ribble Motor Services Ltd. In 1899 the G&KER applied for a line from Pilling to Lancaster.

Another fourteen miles of overhead-trolley tramway to serve Blackpool were authorised in 1901 to the Blackpool and Garstang Light Railway Company, and, if built, would have run from Gynn Square via Layton and Hardhorn to the L&YR station at Singleton, and then across country via Great Eccleston to the LNWR station at Garstang. If this and the other lines mentioned previously had all been built, the Lytham to Fleetwood line would have been the backbone of a network also including lines from Lytham to Southport, Lytham to Preston, Blackpool to Garstang, and Fleetwood to Garstang and Lancaster. The Garstang company changed its name in 1905 to the Blackpool and Fylde Light Railway Company.

The total length of the coastal tramways between Lytham East Beach and Fleetwood Ferry was 18 miles, of which eleven miles are still open. Until 1937 through bookings were available from Lytham to Fleetwood in connection with the daily Isle of Man Steam Packet boat, and through tickets to Douglas could be purchased at the Blackpool tramway offices. In 1936 one car per day was advertised from Lytham to meet the Fleetwood boat, but passengers had to change to a special Blackpool tram at the North Pier, where they alighted to buy their steamer tickets. On reaching Douglas, you can still embark on another long tramride, using the Douglas Corporation horse trams and the connecting electric cars of the Manx Electric Railway to Laxey, Ramsey, and Snaefell Summit.

A dozen miles north-east of Fleetwood we reach Lancaster, where from 1903 to 1930 the Corporation ran 12 standard-gauge single and double-deck trams from the Castle station to Scotforth and to Williamson Park. A separate undertaking was that of the Lancaster and District Tramways Company, whose standard-gauge 1890 horse tramway from Stonewell (near the city centre) through Torrisholme to Morecambe was never electrified, and went over to buses at the end of 1921, later being acquired by a predecessor (Fahy's) of the present Ribble company. For the last year or two, the tramway company ran only a few cars per day, mainly to maintain its franchise.

The Morecambe Tramways Company worked a standard-gauge horse tramway from Strawberry Gardens (Heysham) to East View (Morecambe), of which the section from the boundary at Battery Inn to East View was purchased by Morecambe Corporation in 1908. An extension from East View to Bare was built by the Corporation in 1898, but operated by the company. After achieving the distinction of becoming the last horse tramway in England, this route was replaced by municipal motor buses in 1926. Meanwhile the company had retained the Strawberry Gardens to Battery Inn section, working it latterly with Leyland petrol tramcars, until this was purchased in 1924 by Heysham UDC to scrap, and replaced by buses of Heysham and District Motors, Limited. With the eventual amalgamation of the Heysham Urban District Council with the Borough of Morecambe the new Morecambe and Heysham Corporation took over all local transport in 1929, introducing tickets headed 'Morecambe & Heysham Tramways' although all trams had vanished three years previously. In 1974, local government reorganisation created an enlarged City of Lancaster, whose transport undertaking now covers

The boundary between the Morecambe and Heysham tramways at the Battery Inn, probably in 1924. The Morecambe Corporation horse tram is one of four postwar cars (two double-deckers, and two open toastracks). At the left is one of the four Leyland/ UEC company-owned petrol trams which ran to Strawberry Gardens, Heysham. The bus is a Morecambe Corporation Tilling Stevens. *(Keighley News*

Lancaster, Morecambe, and Heysham, and is the successor to this little tramway network of four distinct undertakings, of which only one was electrified, and whose total route mileage amounted to only eleven. There was also a local electric railway from Lancaster via Morecambe to Heysham, operated by the Midland company and successors from 1908 to 1965, the first in Britain with overhead wires or with high voltage.

On the opposite shore of Morecambe Bay was the isolated tramway system at Barrow-in-Furness, where the British Electric Traction Co Ltd worked 6½ miles on the 4ft gauge, a notable feature of which was the route over the 1909 swing bridge to Walney Island. The BET operated directly, through a local Committee of Management, instead of the normal arrangement through a subsidiary company, but the tramways were taken over by the Barrow-in-Furness Corporation in 1920 and abandoned in 1932. The BET used a mixed fleet of 28 cars of seven different types, to which the Corporation added a further 22 cars of three more types, though there were never more than about 37 in stock at any one time. Three of the same four routes (to Abbey, Roose, and Ramsden Dock, but not Walney Island) were worked from 1885-86 until 1903 by the eight steam locomotives and eight covered-top bogie trailer cars of the Barrow-in-Furness Tramways Co Ltd.

Going north along the Cumbrian coast, through Ravenglass, with its famous 15in gauge Eskdale steam railway, electrification of which was authorised by Act of 1909 but not carried out, we come to Whitehaven, where the West Cumberland Electric Tramways Company was authorised in 1901 to build an ambitious 4ft 8½in gauge line some 31¼ miles long; this was not built, but was to have been Cleator Moor — Hensingham — Whitehaven — Distington — Workington — Low Seaton — Gillhead—Flimby—Maryport—Allonby—Beckfoot—Silloth, with 12¾ miles of reserved track. In the heart of the Lake District, the Windermere and District Electricity Supply Co Ltd applied in 1899 for tramway powers from Windermere railway station to Bowness Pier and Ambleside, following a suggestion two years earlier for a Bowness—Windermere—Ambleside—Grasmere tramway, but in fact no more came of this. The BET had a minority interest in the company, which it soon sold. In 1921 the idea was revived, now to continue to Keswick and use petrol-electric cars.

Finally we come to the most isolated tramway system in Great Britain, that of the City of Carlisle Electric Tramways Co Ltd, whose 3ft 6in gauge routes were fifty miles from any other tramway system. In this important meeting-place of several trunk highways and main railways the local trams ran out to Newtown, Stanwix, Denton Holme, Boundary Road, Warwick Road, and London Road. Operations had started in 1900, with 15 cars, including some single-deckers for the Denton Holme route, which traversed a low bridge. Ownership was complicated, for powers were obtained in 1898 by the Manchester Traction Co Ltd, who also founded Blackpool & Fleetwood. The Carlisle company, which was formed in 1899 to inherit these powers, was controlled additionally by the Dick Kerr, Pritchard Green, and Provincial groups, until its purchase in 1912 by Balfour Beatty, who relaid the track and provided a new fleet of trams. It changed its name in 1926 to the Carlisle and District Transport Co Ltd, and its trams were replaced in 1931 by buses of the Tilling and BET group (chiefly Ribble) when local bus operations were redistributed among five large companies.

Most British steam tramways used top-covered cars, but those at Burnley had open top decks, for which lower fares were charged. These new engines and cars were built by Brush in 1897.
(Tramway and Railway World, June 1897

One of the first 24 electric cars of Burnley Corporation. The next 14 cars had glazed windshields around the upper deck.
(Courtesy A. D. Packer

One of the single deck cars used by Burnley Corporation on the Towneley route. *(TMS*

BURNLEY CORPORATION TRAMWAYS

From 1909, Burnley Corporation's double-deck trams were built (or rebuilt) to the design shown above, with large open balconies flanking a short central upper saloon. The lower left photograph shows the lower saloon of the same car, No. 48.

(Motherwell Library, Hurst Nelson collection

The lower right photograph is of the first of Burnley's two locomotive-type tramway snowploughs. *(TMS*

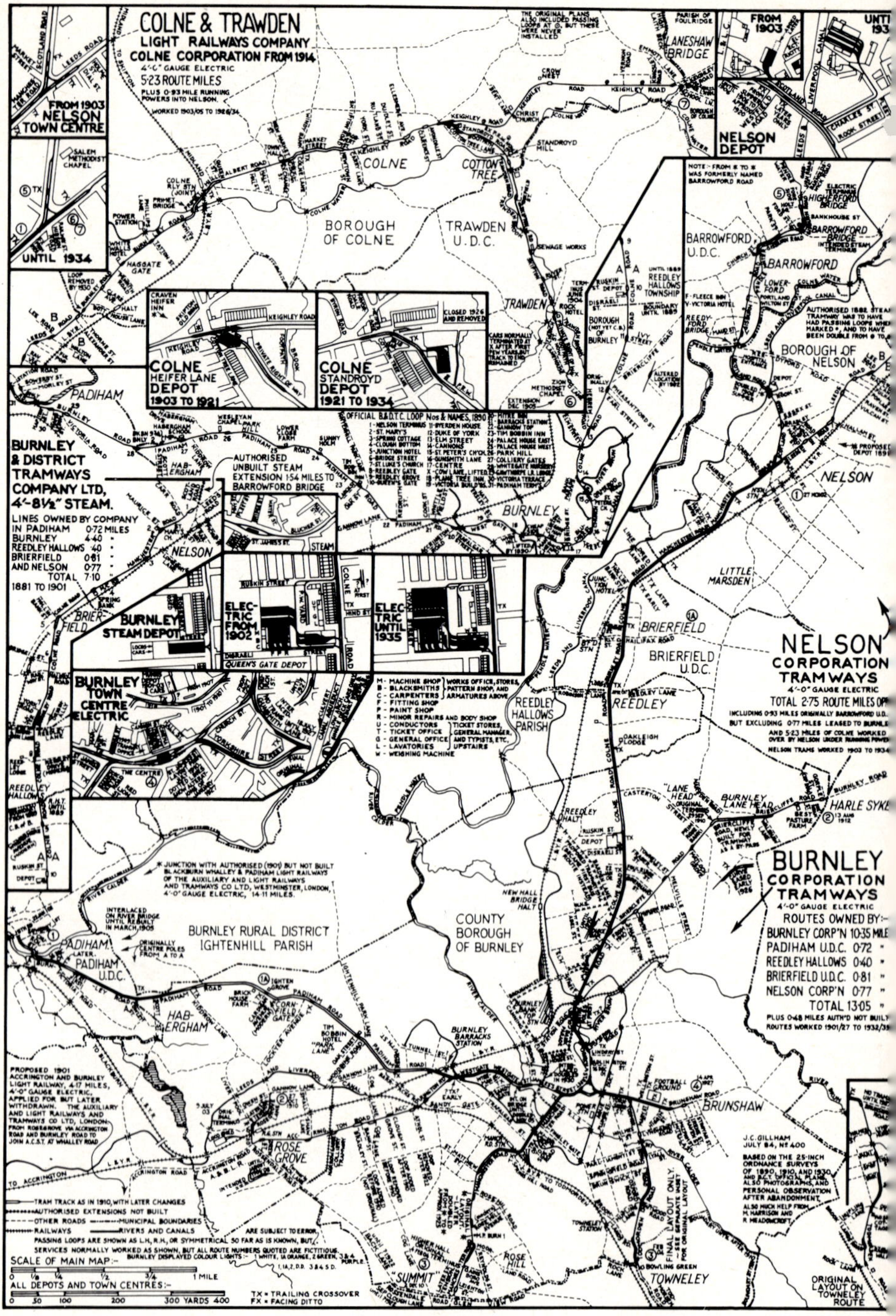
COLNE & TRAWDEN
LIGHT RAILWAYS COMPANY
COLNE CORPORATION FROM 1914
4'-0" GAUGE ELECTRIC
5·23 ROUTE MILES
PLUS 0·93 MILE RUNNING POWERS INTO NELSON.
WORKED 1903/05 TO 1926/34
FROM 1903 NELSON TOWN CENTRE
UNTIL 1934
NELSON DEPOT
LANESHAW BRIDGE
COLNE
COTTON TREE
BOROUGH OF COLNE
TRAWDEN U.D.C.
TRAWDEN
COLNE HEIFER LANE DEPOT 1903 TO 1921
COLNE STANDROYD DEPOT 1921 TO 1934
BARROWFORD U.D.C.
BARROWFORD
BOROUGH OF NELSON
BOROUGH (NOT YET C.B.) OF BURNLEY
REEDLEY HALLOWS TOWNSHIP
PADIHAM
HABERGHAM
BURNLEY & DISTRICT TRAMWAYS COMPANY LTD, 4'-8½" STEAM.
LINES OWNED BY COMPANY
IN PADIHAM 0·72 MILES
BURNLEY 4·40
REEDLEY HALLOWS ·40
BRIERFIELD 0·81
AND NELSON 0·77
TOTAL 7·10
1881 TO 1901
AUTHORISED UNBUILT STEAM EXTENSION 1·54 MILES TO BARROWFORD BRIDGE
OFFICIAL B.&D.T.C. LOOP Nos & NAMES, 1890
BURNLEY
NELSON
BURNLEY STEAM DEPOT
ELECTRIC FROM 1902
ELECTRIC UNTIL 1935
QUEEN'S GATE DEPOT
BURNLEY TOWN CENTRE ELECTRIC
THE CENTRE
M - MACHINE SHOP
B - BLACKSMITHS
C - CARPENTERS
F - FITTING SHOP
P - PAINT SHOP
R - MINOR REPAIRS AND BODY SHOP
U - CONDUCTORS
T - TICKET OFFICE
G - GENERAL OFFICE
L - LAVATORIES
W - WEIGHING MACHINE
WORKS OFFICE, STORES, PATTERN SHOP, AND ARMATURES ABOVE
TICKET STORES, GENERAL MANAGER, AND TYPISTS, ETC. UPSTAIRS
LITTLE MARSDEN
BRIERFIELD
BRIERFIELD U.D.C.
REEDLEY
REEDLEY HALLOWS PARISH
NELSON CORPORATION TRAMWAYS
4'-0" GAUGE ELECTRIC
TOTAL 2·75 ROUTE MILES
NELSON TRAMS WORKED 1903 TO 1934
HARLE SYKE
BURNLEY LANE HEAD
BURNLEY CORPORATION TRAMWAYS
4'-0" GAUGE ELECTRIC
ROUTES OWNED BY:-
BURNLEY CORP'N 10·35 MILES
PADIHAM U.D.C. 0·72
REEDLEY HALLOWS 0·40
BRIERFIELD U.D.C. 0·81
NELSON CORP'N 0·77
TOTAL 13·05
PLUS 0·48 MILES AUTH'D NOT BUILT
ROUTES WORKED 1901/27 TO 1932/35
JUNCTION WITH AUTHORISED (1901) BUT NOT BUILT BLACKBURN WHALLEY & PADIHAM LIGHT RAILWAYS OF THE AUXILIARY AND LIGHT RAILWAYS AND TRAMWAYS CO LTD, WESTMINSTER, LONDON, 4'-0" GAUGE ELECTRIC, 14·11 MILES.
BURNLEY RURAL DISTRICT
IGHTENHILL PARISH
PADIHAM U.D.C.
COUNTY BOROUGH OF BURNLEY
HABERGHAM
PROPOSED 1901 ACCRINGTON AND BURNLEY LIGHT RAILWAY, 4·17 MILES, 4'-0" GAUGE ELECTRIC, APPLIED FOR BUT LATER WITHDRAWN. THE AUXILIARY AND LIGHT RAILWAYS AND TRAMWAYS CO LTD, LONDON.
ROSE GROVE
BRUNSHAW
ROSE HILL
SUMMIT
TOWNELEY
J.C. GILLHAM JULY 84, NT 400
BASED ON THE 25-INCH ORDNANCE SURVEYS OF 1890, 1910 AND 1930, AND B.C.T. OFFICIAL PLANS, ALSO PHOTOGRAPHS AND PERSONAL OBSERVATION AFTER ABANDONMENT.
ALSO MUCH HELP FROM M. HARRISON AND R. MEADOWCROFT
ORIGINAL LAYOUT ON TOWNELEY ROUTE
TRAM TRACK AS IN 1910, WITH LATER CHANGES
AUTHORISED EXTENSIONS NOT BUILT
OTHER ROADS
MUNICIPAL BOUNDARIES
RAILWAYS
RIVERS AND CANALS
PASSING LOOPS ARE SHOWN AS L.H., R.H., OR SYMMETRICAL SO FAR AS IS KNOWN, BUT SERVICES NORMALLY WORKED AS SHOWN, BUT ALL ROUTE NUMBERS QUOTED ARE FICTITIOUS. ARE SUBJECT TO ERROR.
BURNLEY DISPLAYED COLOUR LIGHTS:- 1 WHITE, 1A ORANGE, 2 GREEN, 3 & 4 PURPLE.
SCALE OF MAIN MAP:-
0 1/8 1/4 1/2 3/4 1 MILE
ALL DEPOTS AND TOWN CENTRES:-
0 50 100 200 300 YARDS 400
TX = TRAILING CROSSOVER
FX = FACING DITTO

17

The first six trams of Nelson Corporation were a 4ft. gauge version of a type used in Manchester.
(Courtesy R. Brook)

Nelson Corporation also owned three of these Preston built combination cars of 1903/4, with open sections for smokers.
(UEC Catalogue)

Nelson Corporation low-bridge car 5 at Nelson Centre in 1928.
(Science Museum Whitcombe Collection)

A Colne tram of the 11-12 series, built by Milnes Voss in 1906. Colne Corporation took over the system from the Colne & Trawden company in 1914.
(Courtesy R. Brook)

Two Colne & Trawden cars negotiating the Primet Bridge near Colne station in 1913. This bridge compelled Colne and Nelson to use low-height cars.
(TMS)

For several months in 1934, 30 trams from the Burnley, Colne and Nelson fleets were stored at Burnley's Queensgate depot awaiting buyers. This photograph shows how tall the Burnley trams were compared with those of Nelson and Colne.
(Dr. Hugh Nicol)

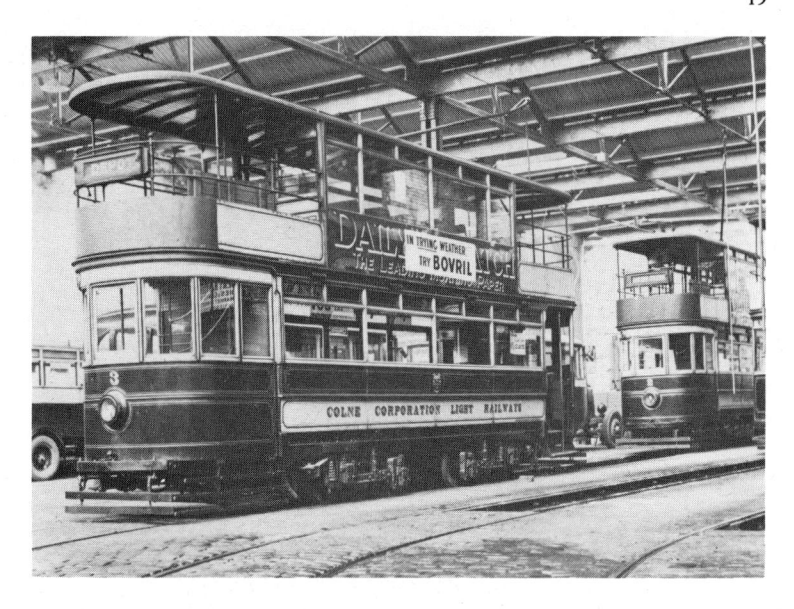

After having taken over the Colne & Trawden Light Railway in 1914, Colne Corporation bought six covered-top trams low enough to pass under the 15ft. 7in. bridge at Colne station. No. 13 was a four-wheel UEC balcony car of 1914, Nos. 2 and 3 were bogie balcony cars built by English Electric in 1920, and Nos. 14-16 were all-enclosed low floor cars built by Brush in 1926, on Peckham Pendulum trucks. Colne 14-16 were the fastest cars in the district. *(Dr. Hugh Nicol; Leicestershire Museums, Brush Collection*

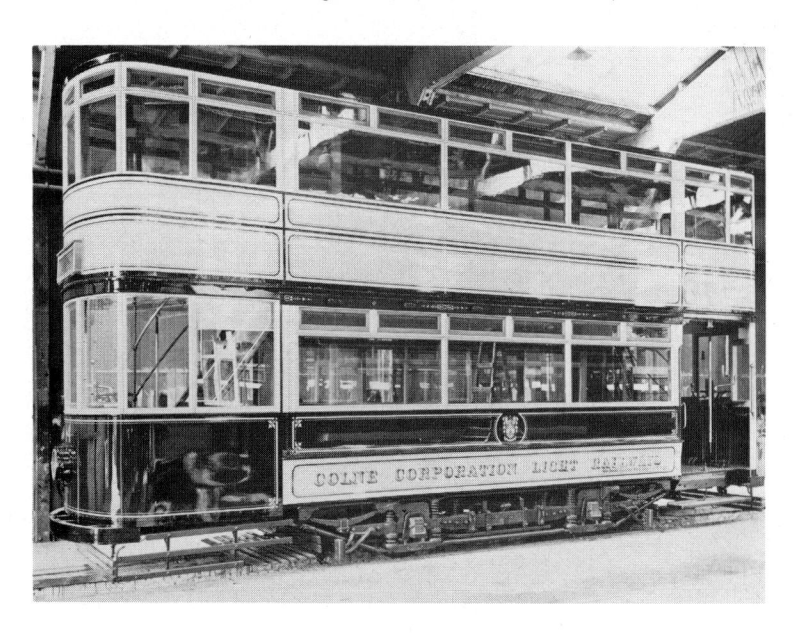

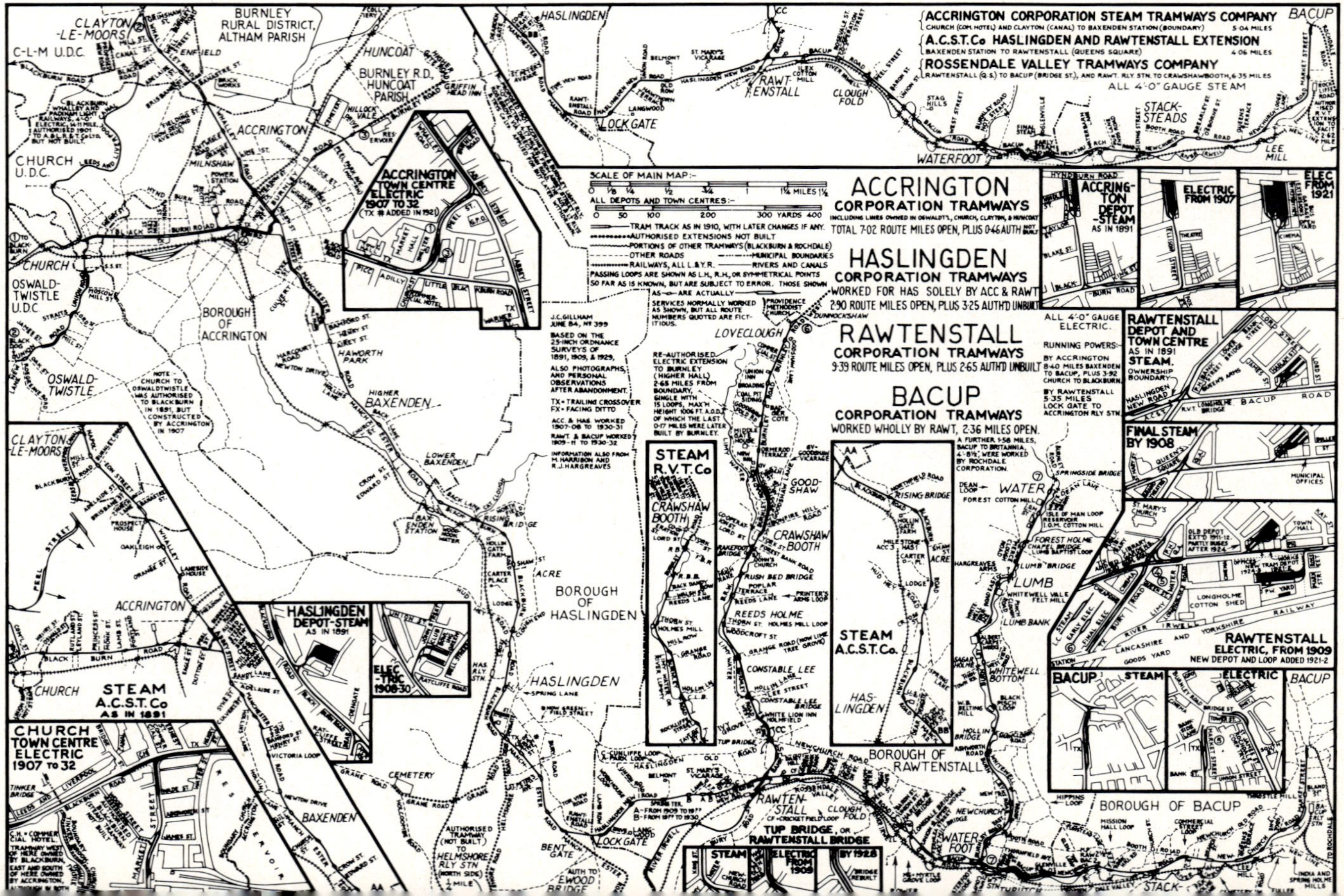

ACCRINGTON CORPORATION STEAM TRAMWAYS COMPANY
CHURCH (COM. HOTEL) AND CLAYTON (CANAL) TO BAXENDEN STATION (BOUNDARY) 5·04 MILES
A.C.S.T.Co HASLINGDEN AND RAWTENSTALL EXTENSION
BAXENDEN STATION TO RAWTENSTALL (QUEENS SQUARE) 4·06 MILES
ROSSENDALE VALLEY TRAMWAYS COMPANY
RAWTENSTALL (Q.S.) TO BACUP (BRIDGE ST.), AND RAWT. RLY STN. TO CRAWSHAWBOOTH, 6·35 MILES
ALL 4'-0" GAUGE STEAM
SCALE OF MAIN MAP:-
ALL DEPOTS AND TOWN CENTRES:-
TRAM TRACK AS IN 1910, WITH LATER CHANGES IF ANY.
AUTHORISED EXTENSIONS NOT BUILT
PORTIONS OF OTHER TRAMWAYS (BLACKBURN & ROCHDALE)
OTHER ROADS
MUNICIPAL BOUNDARIES
RAILWAYS, ALL L.&Y.R.
RIVERS AND CANALS
PASSING LOOPS ARE SHOWN AS L.H, R.H, OR SYMMETRICAL POINTS SO FAR AS IS KNOWN, BUT ARE SUBJECT TO ERROR. THOSE SHOWN AS —ARE ACTUALLY
SERVICES NORMALLY WORKED AS SHOWN, BUT ALL ROUTE NUMBERS QUOTED ARE FICTITIOUS.
ACCRINGTON
CORPORATION TRAMWAYS
INCLUDING LINES OWNED IN OSWALDTS., CHURCH, CLAYTON, & HUNCOAT
TOTAL 7·02 ROUTE MILES OPEN, PLUS 0·46 AUTH NOT BUILT
HASLINGDEN
CORPORATION TRAMWAYS
WORKED FOR HAS SOLELY BY ACC & RAWT
2·90 ROUTE MILES OPEN, PLUS 3·25 AUTH'D UNBUILT
RAWTENSTALL
CORPORATION TRAMWAYS
9·39 ROUTE MILES OPEN, PLUS 2·65 AUTH'D UNBUILT
BACUP
CORPORATION TRAMWAYS
WORKED WHOLLY BY RAWT, 2·36 MILES OPEN.
A FURTHER 1·58 MILES, BACUP TO BRITANNIA, 4'-8½", WERE WORKED BY ROCHDALE CORPORATION.
ALL 4'-0" GAUGE ELECTRIC.
RUNNING POWERS:-
BY ACCRINGTON 8·40 MILES BAXENDEN TO BACUP, PLUS 3·92 CHURCH TO BLACKBURN.
BY RAWTENSTALL 5·35 MILES LOCK GATE TO ACCRINGTON RLY STN.
J.C.GILLHAM
JUNE 84, Nº 399
BASED ON THE 25-INCH ORDNANCE SURVEYS OF 1891, 1909, & 1929,
ALSO PHOTOGRAPHS, AND PERSONAL OBSERVATIONS AFTER ABANDONMENT.
TX = TRAILING CROSSOVER
FX = FACING DITTO
ACC. & HAS WORKED 1907-08 TO 1930-31
RAWT. & BACUP WORKED 1909-11 TO 1930-32
INFORMATION ALSO FROM M. HARRISON AND R.J. HARGREAVES
RE-AUTHORISED ELECTRIC EXTENSION TO BURNLEY (HIGHER HALL) 2·65 MILES FROM BOUNDARY, SINGLE WITH 15 LOOPS, MAX'M HEIGHT 1006 FT. A.O.D., OF WHICH THE LAST 0·17 MILES WERE LATER BUILT BY BURNLEY.
NOTE - CHURCH TO OSWALDTWISTLE WAS AUTHORISED TO BLACKBURN IN 1891, BUT CONSTRUCTED BY ACCRINGTON IN 1907
ACCRINGTON TOWN CENTRE ELECTRIC 1907 TO 32
(TX # ADDED IN 1921)
ACCRINGTON DEPOT - STEAM AS IN 1891
ELECTRIC FROM 1907
ELEC FROM 1921
RAWTENSTALL DEPOT AND TOWN CENTRE AS IN 1891 STEAM.
FINAL STEAM BY 1908
RAWTENSTALL ELECTRIC, FROM 1909
NEW DEPOT AND LOOP ADDED 1921-2
BACUP STEAM
ELECTRIC
STEAM R.V.T.Co
STEAM A.C.S.T.Co.
HASLINGDEN DEPOT-STEAM AS IN 1891
ELEC-TRIC 1908-30
STEAM A.C.S.T.Co AS IN 1891
CHURCH TOWN CENTRE ELECTRIC 1907 TO 32
TUP BRIDGE, OR RAWTENSTALL BRIDGE
STEAM
ELECTRIC FROM 1909
BY 1928
BOROUGH OF ACCRINGTON
BOROUGH OF HASLINGDEN
BOROUGH OF RAWTENSTALL
BOROUGH OF BACUP
BURNLEY RURAL DISTRICT, ALTHAM PARISH
BURNLEY R.D., HUNCOAT PARISH
CHURCH U.D.C.
OSWALDTWISTLE U.D.C.
C-L-M U.D.C.
CLAYTON-LE-MOORS
ACCRINGTON
HUNCOAT
CHURCH
OSWALDTWISTLE
HASLINGDEN
RAWTENSTALL
BACUP
WATERFOOT
STACKSTEADS
LOCK GATE
CLOUGH FOLD
HIGHER BAXENDEN
LOWER BAXENDEN
BAXENDEN
LOVECLOUGH
GOODSHAW
CRAWSHAW BOOTH
REEDS HOLME
CONSTABLE LEE
LUMB
WATER
WHITEWELL BOTTOM
LEE MILL
CEMETERY
AUTHORISED TRAMWAY (NOT BUILT) TO HELMSHORE RLY STN

21

A Thomas Green engine and G. F. Milnes car of the Rossendale Valley Tramways Company. Steam trams ran between Bacup and Rawtenstall from 1889 to 1909. *(TMS*

For a few months in 1908, Haslingden Corporation ran its own steam tram service with engines and cars bought from Accrington Corporation. This scene at Haslingden Centre shows a trailer car consisting apparently of an Ashbury top deck on a Falcon lower deck, both second-hand.
(Courtesy D. Tudor

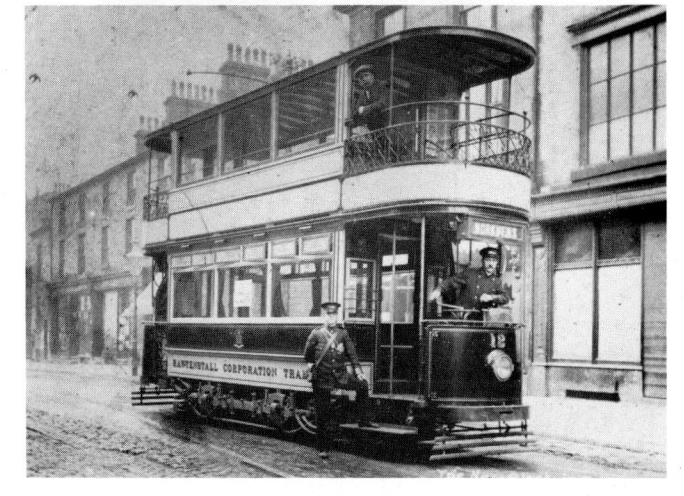

One of Rawtenstall Corporation's first electric cars, built at Preston in 1909. They originally had regenerative equipment. *(TMS*

Two trams numbered 20 seen together at Waterfoot in 1911. The double-decker is an Accrington car on the through service from Accrington to Bacup, the single-decker is Rawtenstall 20 on the Lumb Valley route to Water.
(Courtesy M. Harrison)

Rawtenstall steam tram engine 6, bogie electric car 26 and a new Leyland bus at the depot six days after the last tram ran on 31 March 1932. *(Courtesy C. S. Dunbar)*

Rawtenstall's electric trams were bought by a scrap firm, A. Devey & Co., who sent photographs of them to likely buyers. They offered eight bogie cars, two enclosed four-wheelers and six open-balcony four-wheelers.
(Courtesy R. Brook)

23

Breaking up the Accrington steam trams in July, 1907, after electric services began. The steam trams were known locally as the Baltic Fleet.
(Courtesy A. D. Packer)

A coloured commercial postcard of one of Accrington's new electric trams in 1907.
(Constantine Series, J. H. Price collection)

Accrington's first electric trams included four single-deckers for the route to Oswaldtwistle. As built, they had three compartments, but the inner partitions were later removed.
(Lens of Sutton

Accrington Corporation's first two bogie double-deck cars, 38 and 39, were built by the Brush Electrical Engineering Co. Ltd. in 1915, the year of this official Brush photograph. Two similar cars were built in 1920. After Accrington closed its tramways in 1932, one was sold to Lytham St. Annes and the other three to Southend-on-Sea. All four had to be re-gauged. *(Leicestershire Museums, Brush Collection)*

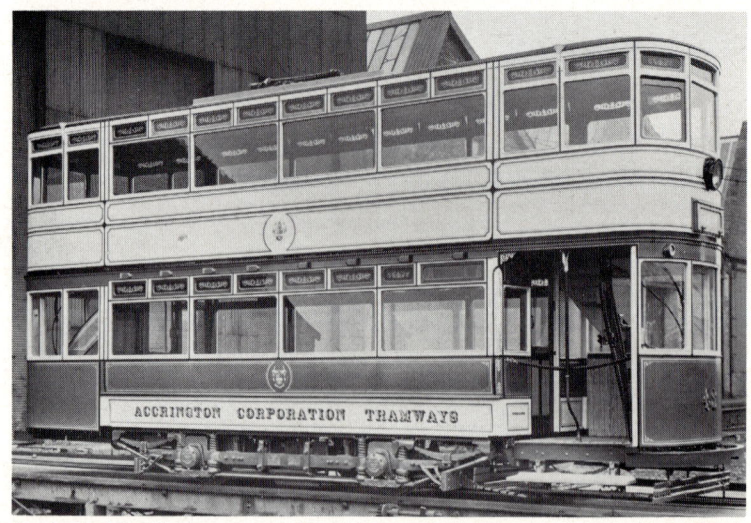

Accrington's last two new trams, 42 and 43, were lowbridge cars of 1926 with the Brush company's patented low-floor construction; 43 is seen here at the maker's works in Loughborough. These two cars were sold in 1931 to Sunderland Corporation.
(Leicestershire Museums, Brush Collection)

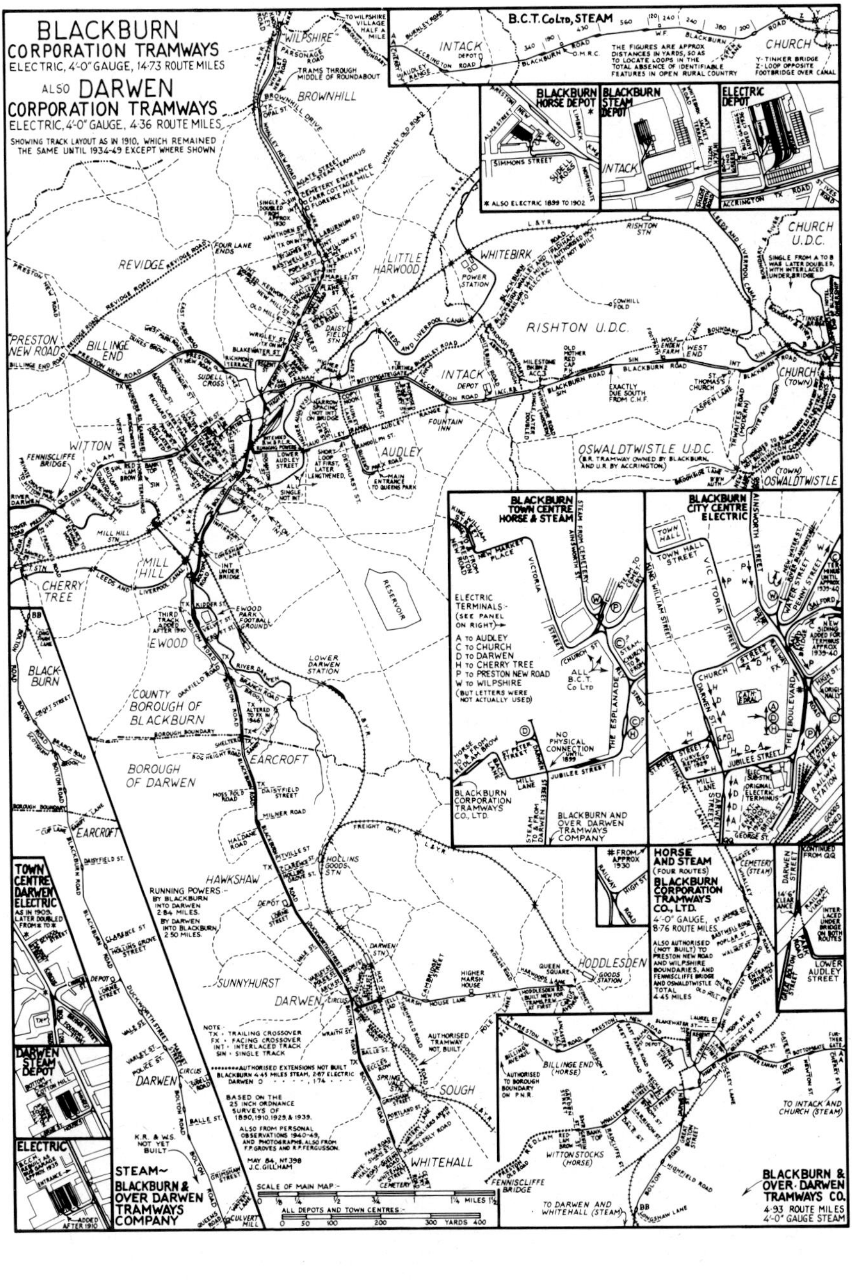

BLACKBURN CORPORATION TRAMWAYS
ELECTRIC, 4'-0" GAUGE, 14·73 ROUTE MILES
ALSO DARWEN CORPORATION TRAMWAYS
ELECTRIC, 4'-0" GAUGE, 4·36 ROUTE MILES
SHOWING TRACK LAYOUT AS IN 1910, WHICH REMAINED THE SAME UNTIL 1934-49 EXCEPT WHERE SHOWN
B.C.T. Co LTD, STEAM
THE FIGURES ARE APPROX DISTANCES IN YARDS, SO AS TO LOCATE LOOPS IN THE TOTAL ABSENCE OF IDENTIFIABLE FEATURES IN OPEN RURAL COUNTRY
Y - TINKER BRIDGE
Z - LOOP OPPOSITE FOOTBRIDGE OVER CANAL
INTACK
CHURCH
BLACKBURN HORSE DEPOT
BLACKBURN STEAM DEPOT
ELECTRIC DEPOT
SIMMONS STREET
* ALSO ELECTRIC 1899 TO 1902
WILPSHIRE
BROWNHILL
TRAMS THROUGH MIDDLE OF ROUNDABOUT
REVIDGE
LITTLE HARWOOD
WHITEBIRK
POWER STATION
RISHTON STN
CHURCH U.D.C.
SINGLE FROM A TO B WAS LATER DOUBLED, WITH INTERLACED UNDER BRIDGE
RISHTON U.D.C.
PRESTON NEW ROAD
BILLINGE END
SUDELL CROSS
INTACK DEPOT
EXACTLY DUE SOUTH FROM C.H.F.
CHURCH (TOWN)
FOUNTAIN INN
OSWALDTWISTLE U.D.C.
(B.R. TRAMWAY OWNED BY BLACKBURN, AND U.R. BY ACCRINGTON)
(TOWN) OSWALDTWISTLE
WITTON
FENNISCLIFFE BRIDGE
AUDLEY
MAIN ENTRANCE TO QUEENS PARK
RIVER DARWEN
MILL HILL
CHERRY TREE
LEEDS AND LIVERPOOL CANAL
RESERVOIR
EWOOD
EWOOD PARK FOOTBALL GROUND
LOWER DARWEN STATION
COUNTY BOROUGH OF BLACKBURN
BOROUGH OF DARWEN
EARCROFT
BLACKBURN TOWN CENTRE HORSE & STEAM
ELECTRIC TERMINALS:- (SEE PANEL ON RIGHT)
A TO AUDLEY
C TO CHURCH
D TO DARWEN
H TO CHERRY TREE
P TO PRESTON NEW ROAD
W TO WILPSHIRE
(BUT LETTERS WERE NOT ACTUALLY USED)
ALL B.C.T. Co LTD
NO PHYSICAL CONNECTION UNTIL 1899
BLACKBURN CORPORATION TRAMWAYS CO., LTD.
BLACKBURN AND OVER DARWEN TRAMWAYS COMPANY
BLACKBURN CITY CENTRE ELECTRIC
TOWN HALL
HAWKSHAW
RUNNING POWERS:- BY BLACKBURN INTO DARWEN 2·84 MILES. BY DARWEN INTO BLACKBURN 2·50 MILES.
HOLLINS GOODS STN
DARWEN STN
HODDLESDEN
SUNNYHURST
DARWEN
HIGHER MARSH HOUSE
AUTHORISED TRAMWAY NOT BUILT
SOUGH
WHITEHALL
TOWN CENTRE DARWEN ELECTRIC
DARWEN STEAM DEPOT
ELECTRIC
ADDED AFTER 1910
NOTE:- TX - TRAILING CROSSOVER FX - FACING CROSSOVER INT - INTERLACED TRACK SIN - SINGLE TRACK
AUTHORISED EXTENSIONS NOT BUILT BLACKBURN 4·45 MILES STEAM, 2·87 ELECTRIC DARWEN 1·74
BASED ON THE 25 INCH ORDNANCE SURVEYS OF 1890, 1910, 1929 & 1939.
ALSO FROM PERSONAL OBSERVATIONS 1940-49, AND PHOTOGRAPHS, ALSO FROM F.P. GROVES AND R.P. FERGUSSON.
MAY 84, Nº 398 J.C. GILLHAM
K.R. & W.S. NOT YET BUILT
STEAM~ BLACKBURN & OVER DARWEN TRAMWAYS COMPANY
SCALE OF MAIN MAP:- 0 1/8 1/4 1/2 3/4 1 1 1/4 MILES 1 1/2
ALL DEPOTS AND TOWN CENTRES:- 0 50 100 200 300 YARDS 400
HORSE AND STEAM (FOUR ROUTES) BLACKBURN CORPORATION TRAMWAYS CO., LTD.
4'-0" GAUGE, 8·76 ROUTE MILES.
ALSO AUTHORISED (NOT BUILT) TO PRESTON NEW ROAD AND WILPSHIRE BOUNDARIES, AND FENNISCLIFFE BRIDGE AND OSWALDTWISTLE TOTAL 4·45 MILES
LOWER AUDLEY STREET
BILLINGE END (HORSE)
AUTHORISED TO BOROUGH BOUNDARY ON P.N.R.
WITTON STOCKS (HORSE)
TO INTACK AND CHURCH (STEAM)
TO DARWEN AND WHITEHALL (STEAM)
BLACKBURN & OVER DARWEN TRAMWAYS CO.
4·93 ROUTE MILES 4'-0" GAUGE STEAM

The Blackburn and Over Darwen Tramways were the first in Britain to be authorised exclusively for steam traction. The first trailer cars were of the single-ended Eades Patent Reversible type.
(TMS

Blackburn Corporation's permanent-way car hauling rails at Darwen Boundary in 1926.
(Science Museum, Whitcombe Collection

Darwen 7 and a Blackburn tram at Blackburn railway station about 1938, terminus of the joint service between the two towns.

Two Blackburn trams on the Church route in 1947. Blackburn's trams ran through to Accrington via Church from 1907 until 1931, and Accrington trams shared in the service from 1917.
(N. N. Forbes)

The Blackburn tram fleet included 12 single-deck cars which were used mainly on the Audley route.
(Science Museum, Whitcombe Collection)

The scene inside Blackburn's Intack depot on 16 July 1947.
(D. Conrad)

A Darwen Corporation car, probably No. 1, decorated for the Coronation in June 1911. *(TMS*

Darwen 11 at the terminus of the steep Hoddlesden route. This car was destroyed in a runaway accident in September 1926 and later replaced by a car bought from Rawtenstall.
(A. J. Evans)

Darwen 23 at Whitehall terminus in 1937. Darwen's two streamlined trams (23 and 24) were known locally as 'Queen Mary' and 'Queen Elizabeth'. They were sold to Llandudno in 1946.
(W. A. Camwell)

29

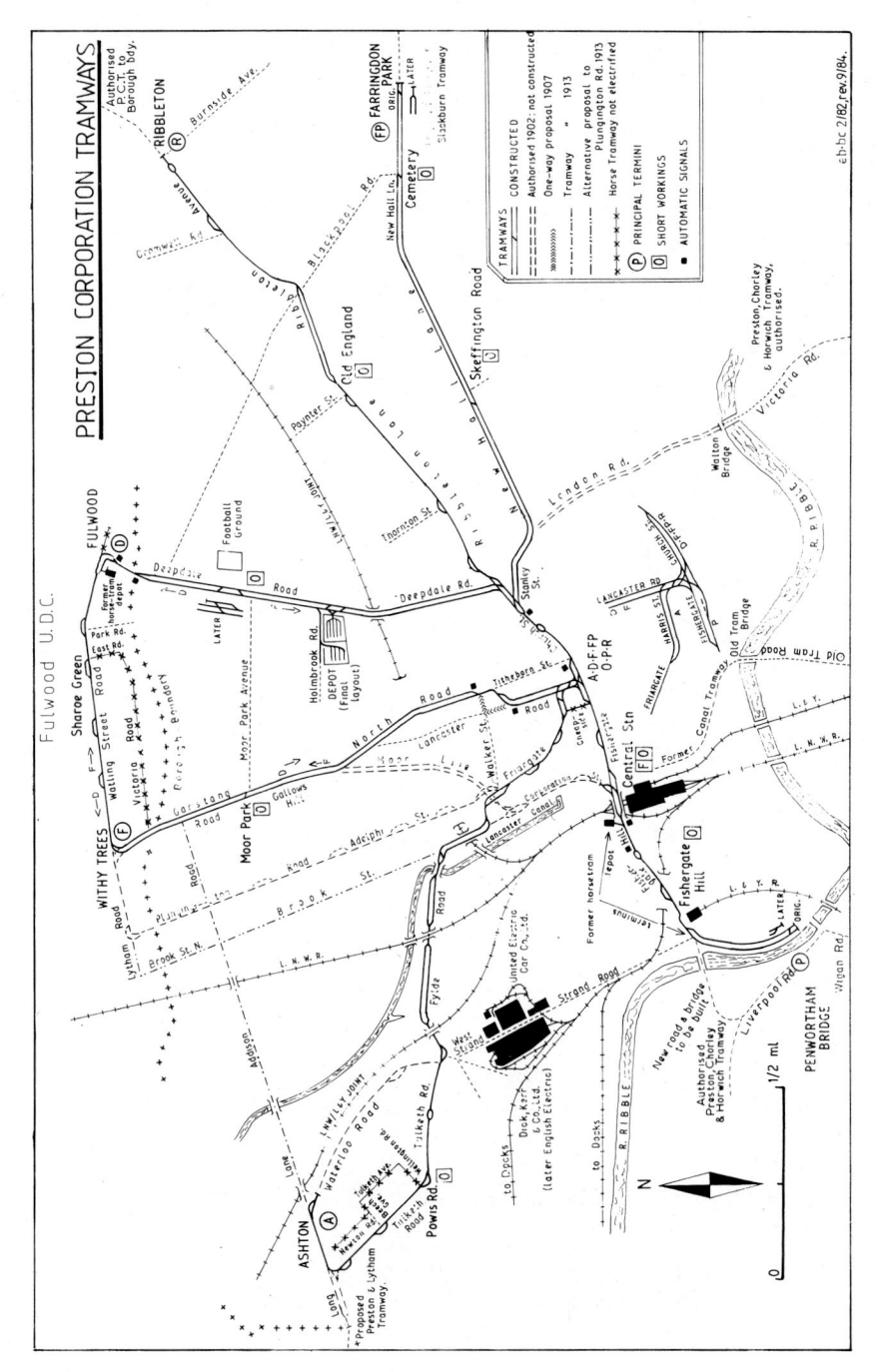

A Preston horse tram at Fulwood terminus on its last day, 31 December 1903. The window poster announces an auction of the 80 horses. *(TMS*

One of the first Preston electric trams, June 1904. A later view of one of these cars appears on page 8.
(T. J. Calvert

The last new trams to enter service at Preston were three enclosed cars built in 1928/29. One was later sold to Lytham St. Annes. This photograph was taken at Ashton terminus on 27 June 1934.
(R. Elliott

31

One of the gas-engined trams of the Blackpool, St. Annes & Lytham Tramways Co. which ran from 1897 to 1903.
(TMS

The Lytham company electrified its routes in 1903 and ran a through service to Blackpool. The lines were municipalised in 1920.

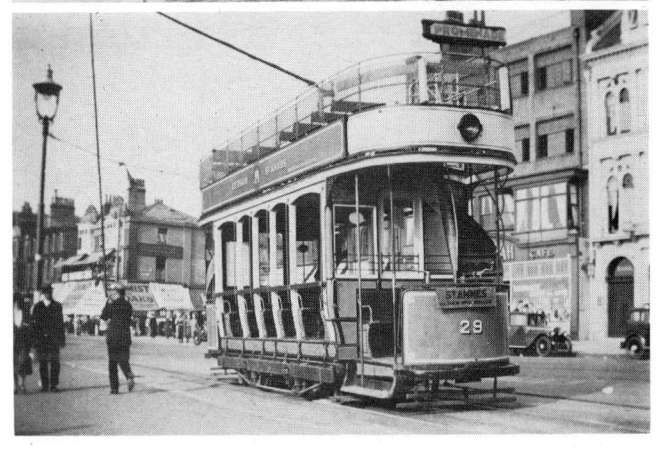

Twenty Lytham trams were of this unusual design with cross-bench lower decks. This photograph was taken in August 1933.
(M. J. O'Connor

32

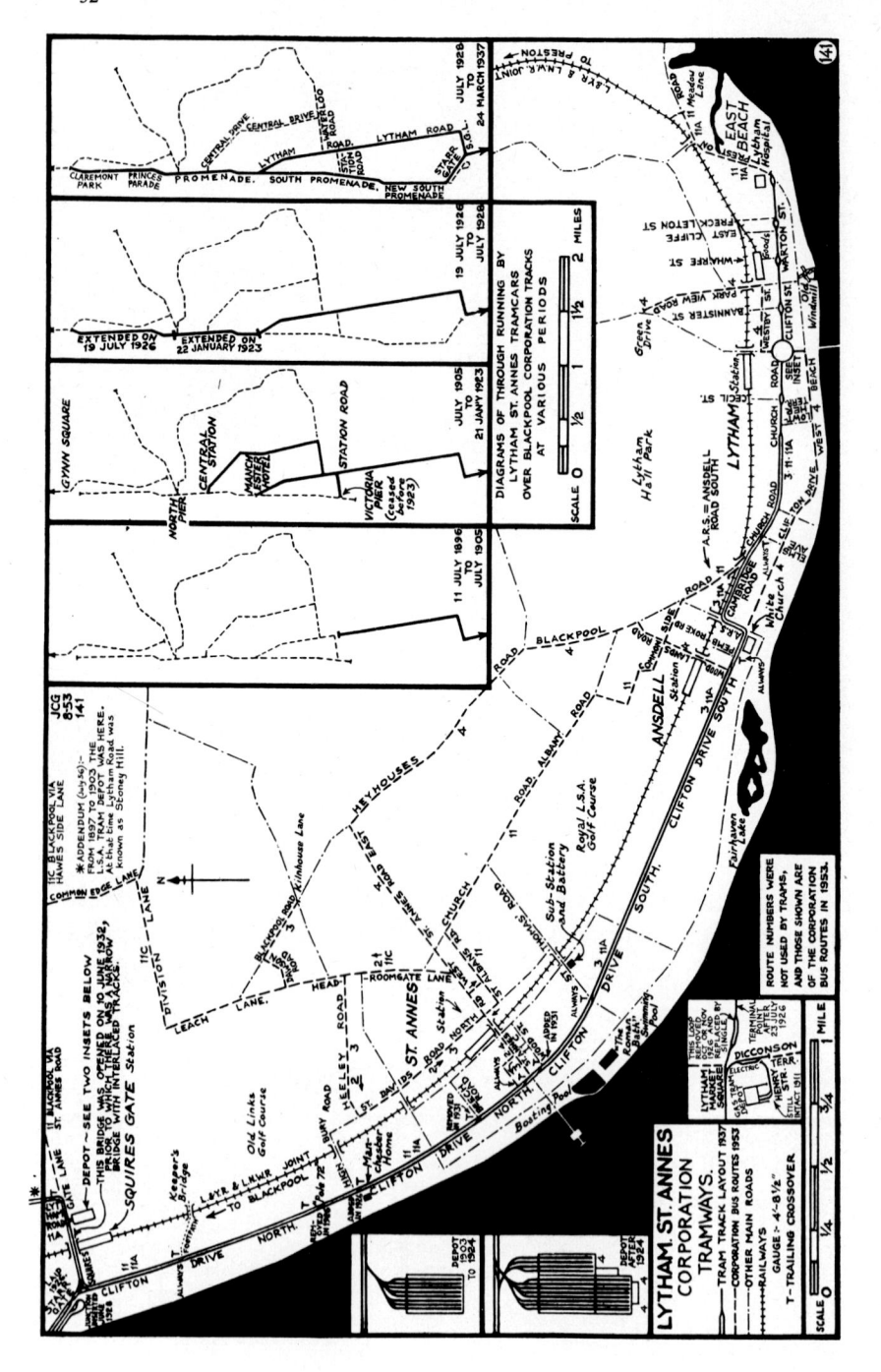

A Lytham tram of series 41-50, built by English Electric in 1924. They were known as the Lytham Pullmans from their comfortable leather seats.
(M. J. O'Connor)

In 1933 Lytham St. Annes Corporation bought four single-deck cars from the Dearne District Light Railway in South Yorkshire.
(R. Wilson)

Lytham's largest tram was No. 55, bought in 1933 from Accrington. See also page 24.
(Courtesy D. Gill)

Blackpool's trams owe their survival to the fine promenade reserved trac

The map below shows the tramways (and railways) as they existed

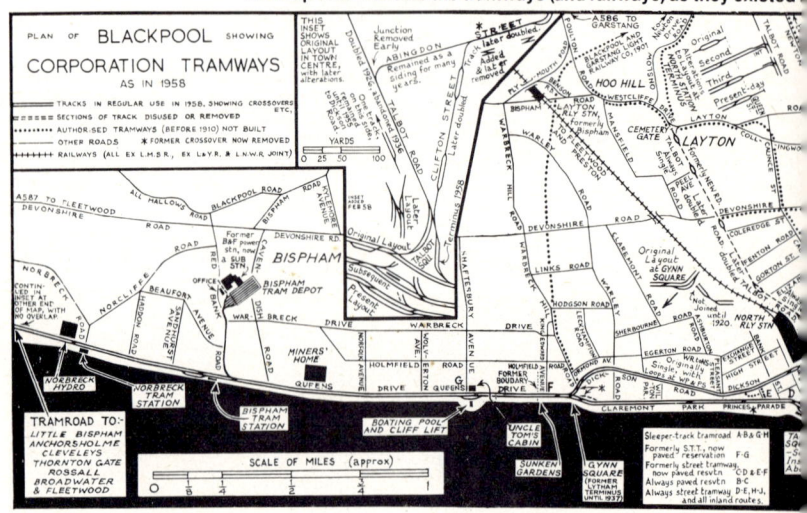

...re in the 1950s with a 304-328 class car.   *(Valentine & Sons)*

...fore the closure of Central Station and the street tramway routes.

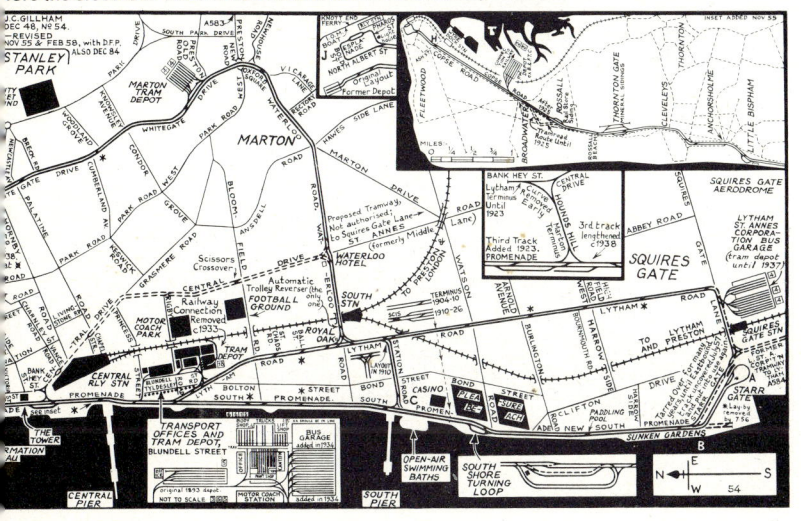

Blackpool conduit car No. 10 at the entrance to Blundell Street depot in about 1894. The underground conduit supply was replaced by overhead wires in 1899. *(TMS*

Ex-conduit car 4 of 1885 was used as an overhead repair car until the 1930s and was then stored as a relic. *(TMS*

In 1960 No. 4 was restored for the 75th Anniversary procesion and renumbered 1. Another car restored was Blackpool & Fleetwood saloon No. 40, seen at the left.
(J. H. Price)

Blackpool trams were for many years among the most profitable in Britain. The four-staircase Dreadnought cars were specially designed for the Promenade route.
(Victoria Real Photo Series

Blackpool toast-rack 69 picking up a load of holidaymakers in Talbot Square in 1911. The pre-1914 tour fare was fourpence.
(TMS

A Blackpool photographer, Mr. Wiggins, would take photographs of each circular tour car near the Oxford Hotel, Marton, and take orders for the prints.
(J. H. Price collection

Above: Standard balcony car No. 40, just repainted in the then-new green livery. The previous Corporation livery was red, white and teak.

(Science Museum, Whitcombe Collection)

BLACKPOOL IN 1934

Below: The inaugural press trip of Blackpool's new streamlined trams on 19 March 1934. Open-top car 226 (later renumbered 237), open 'boat' car 225, and railcoach 224, all newly built by English Electric at Preston.   *(Fox Photos)*

39

The last streamlined trams added to the prewar Blackpool fleet were Sun Saloons 10-21 of 1939, later known as the Marton Vambacs from their postwar equipment.
(English Electric

During the war the open-top double-deck cars were enclosed, and most Blackpool trams were in a mainly-green livery. This one is 263 at Rigby Road depot in July 1945.
(D. Conrad

Prototype new double-decker 761, built by Blackpool Transport in 1979. No. 762 is similar but has a centre exit.
(G. S. Palmer

Blackpool Illuminated Trams

No account of Blackpool's trams would be complete without some of the famous tableau cars which run during the Autumn Illuminations. These three are the Gondola (1927 to 1962), the Rocket (1961) and the Western Train (1962). A full list appears on page 57.

(D. Tate (centre), J. H. Price

41

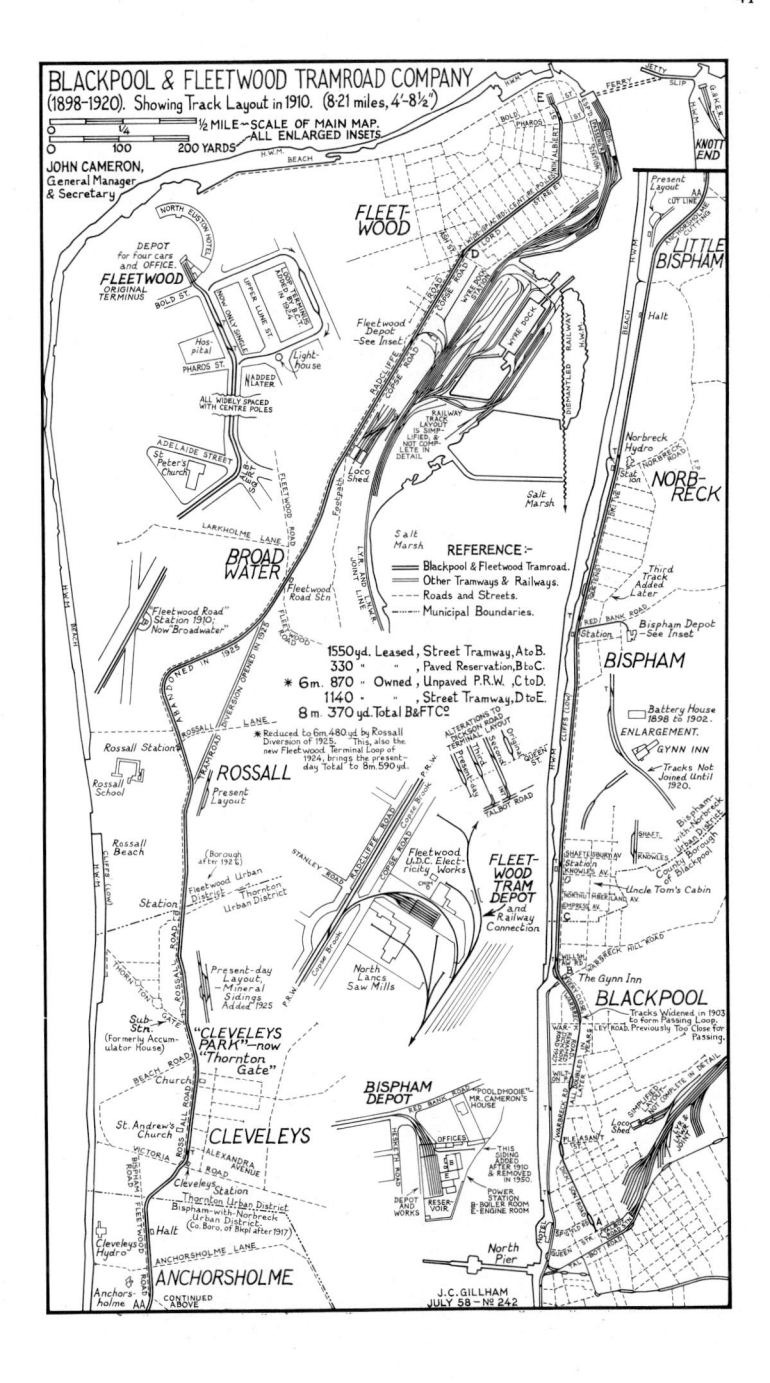

BLACKPOOL TO FLEETWOOD

The Blackpool terminus of the Blackpool and Fleetwood Tramroad in Dickson Road, about 1902.
(Lens of Sutton)

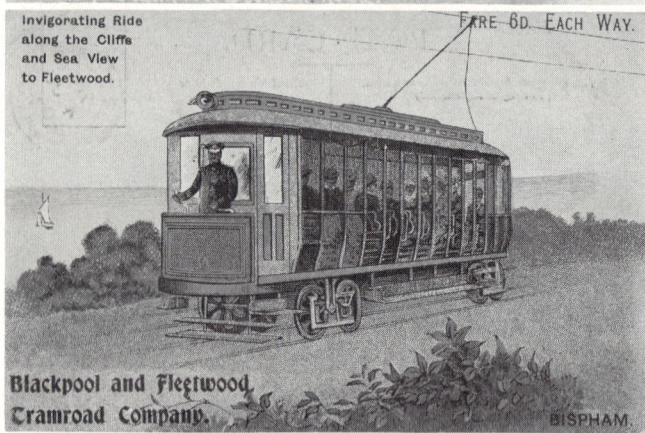

An official coloured postcard of Blackpool and Fleetwood 33 sold by the Tramroad Company. This example is postmarked July 1905.
(J. H. Price collection)

Bispham in 1905, with crossbench and saloon cars of the Blackpool and Fleetwood Tramroad Company. *(Courtesy G. L. Gundry)*

43

In May, 1924, Blackpool trams 121 and 122 (the former Tramroad cars 33 and 34) were used by English Electric to test multiple-unit equipment.
(GEC Traction Ltd

Mainstay of the Fleetwood route for many years were Blackpool Corporation's 'Pantograph' class cars 167 to 176. This photograph shows car 169 at Little Bispham in 1960.
(A. D. Packer

The inaugural run of Blackpool's first twin-car set on 9 April 1958. Ten new trailers were bought in 1960-61.
(D. F. Phillips

The Blackpool-Fleetwood route is now worked mainly by these one-man trams rebuilt in the Corporation's workshop in 1972-76 from vehicles built in 1934-35.
(T. Walmsley

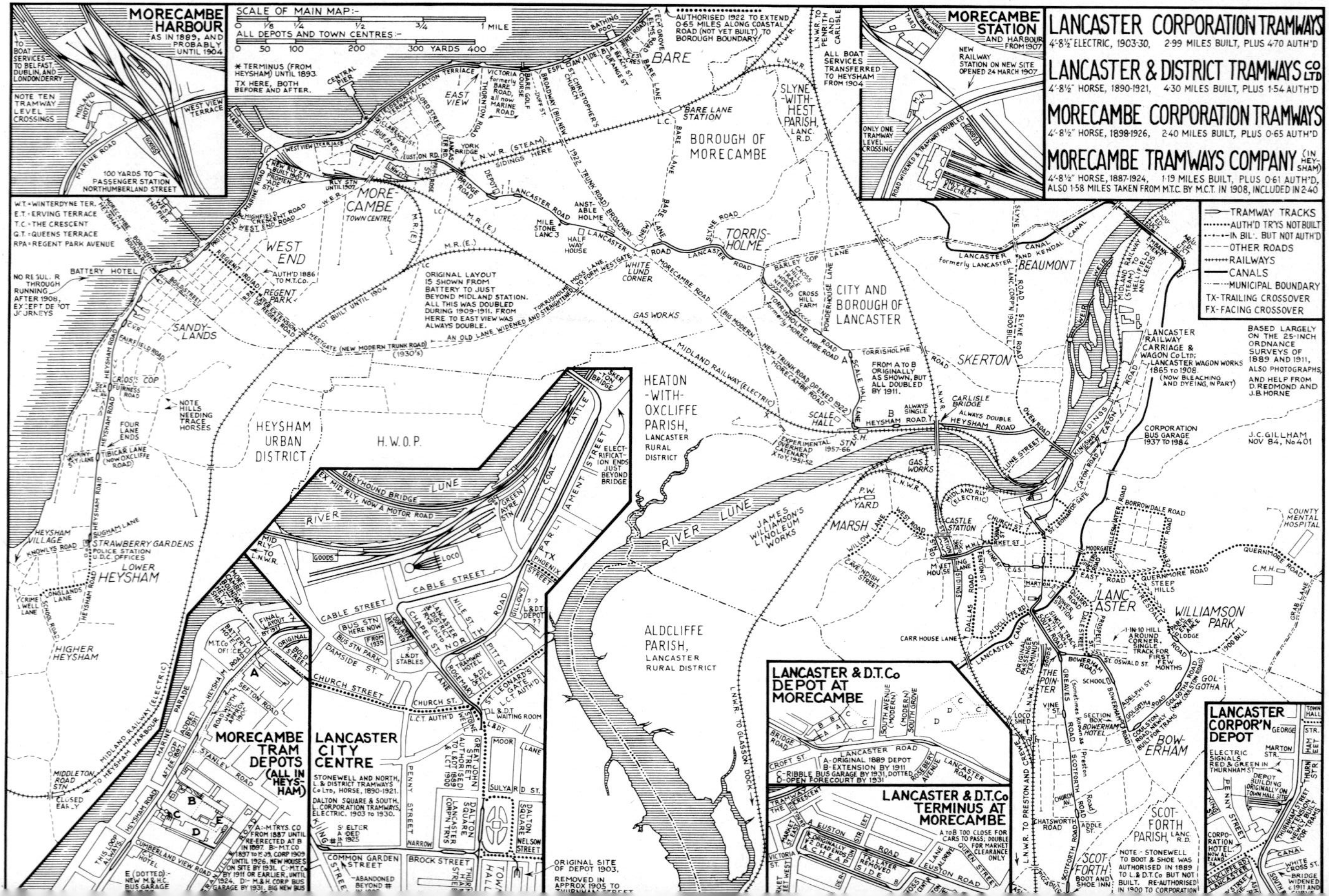
LANCASTER CORPORATION TRAMWAYS
4'-8½" ELECTRIC, 1903-30, 2·99 MILES BUILT, PLUS 4·70 AUTH'D
LANCASTER & DISTRICT TRAMWAYS Co LTD
4'-8½" HORSE, 1890-1921, 4·30 MILES BUILT, PLUS 1·54 AUTH'D
MORECAMBE CORPORATION TRAMWAYS
4'-8½" HORSE, 1898-1926, 2·40 MILES BUILT, PLUS 0·65 AUTH'D
MORECAMBE TRAMWAYS COMPANY (IN HEYSHAM)
4'-8½" HORSE, 1887-1924, 1·19 MILES BUILT, PLUS 0·61 AUTH'D, ALSO 1·58 MILES TAKEN FROM M.T.C. BY M.C.T. IN 1908, INCLUDED IN 2·40
TRAMWAY TRACKS
AUTH'D TR'YS NOT BUILT
IN BILL BUT NOT AUTH'D
OTHER ROADS
RAILWAYS
CANALS
MUNICIPAL BOUNDARY
TX-TRAILING CROSSOVER
FX-FACING CROSSOVER
BASED LARGELY ON THE 25-INCH ORDNANCE SURVEYS OF 1889 AND 1911, ALSO PHOTOGRAPHS, AND HELP FROM D.REDMOND AND J.B.HORNE
J.C.GILLHAM NOV 84, No 401
SCALE OF MAIN MAP:-
0 1/8 1/4 1/2 3/4 1 MILE
ALL DEPOTS AND TOWN CENTRES:-
0 50 100 200 300 YARDS 400
* TERMINUS (FROM HEYSHAM) UNTIL 1893.
TX HERE, BOTH BEFORE AND AFTER.
MORECAMBE HARBOUR
AS IN 1889, AND PROBABLY UNTIL 1904
TO BOAT SERVICES TO BELFAST, DUBLIN, AND LONDONDERRY
NOTE TEN TRAMWAY LEVEL CROSSINGS
100 YARDS TO PASSENGER STATION NORTHUMBERLAND STREET
MORECAMBE STATION AND HARBOUR FROM 1907
NEW RAILWAY STATION ON NEW SITE OPENED 24 MARCH 1907
ONLY ONE TRAMWAY LEVEL CROSSING
ALL BOAT SERVICES TRANSFERRED TO HEYSHAM FROM 1904
AUTHORISED 1922 TO EXTEND 0·65 MILES ALONG COASTAL ROAD (NOT YET BUILT) TO BOROUGH BOUNDARY
W.T.=WINTERDYNE TER.
E.T.=ERVING TERRACE
T.C.=THE CRESCENT
Q.T.=QUEENS TERRACE
RPA=REGENT PARK AVENUE
NO REGULAR THROUGH RUNNING AFTER 1908, EXCEPT DEPOT JOURNEYS
BOROUGH OF MORECAMBE
CITY AND BOROUGH OF LANCASTER
HEYSHAM URBAN DISTRICT
H.W.O.P.
HEATON -WITH- OXCLIFFE PARISH, LANCASTER RURAL DISTRICT
ALDCLIFFE PARISH, LANCASTER RURAL DISTRICT
SLYNE -WITH- HEST PARISH, LANC. R.D.
SCOT- FORTH PARISH, LANC. R.D.
ORIGINAL LAYOUT IS SHOWN FROM BATTERY TO JUST BEYOND MIDLAND STATION. ALL THIS WAS DOUBLED DURING 1909-1911. FROM HERE TO EAST VIEW WAS ALWAYS DOUBLE.
AN OLD LANE WIDENED AND STRAIGHTENED
FROM A TO B ORIGINALLY AS SHOWN, BUT ALL DOUBLED BY 1911.
NOTE HILLS NEEDING TRACE HORSES
CORPORATION BUS GARAGE 1937 TO 1984
LANCASTER RAILWAY CARRIAGE & WAGON Co LTD; LANCASTER WAGON WORKS 1865 to 1908 (NOW BLEACHING AND DYEING, IN PART)
EXPERIMENTAL OVERHEAD CATENARY X to Y, 1951-52
1-IN-10 HILL AROUND CORNER. SINGLE TRACK FOR FIRST FEW MONTHS
NOTE:- STONEWELL TO BOOT & SHOE WAS AUTHORISED IN 1889 TO L.& D.T.Co BUT NOT BUILT. RE-AUTHORISED IN 1900 TO CORPORATION
MORECAMBE TRAM DEPOTS (ALL IN HEYSHAM)
LANCASTER CITY CENTRE
STONEWELL AND NORTH, L. & DISTRICT TRAMWAYS Co LTD, HORSE, 1890-1921.
DALTON SQUARE & SOUTH, L. CORPORATION TRAMWAYS, ELECTRIC. 1903 to 1930.
GREAT JOHN STREET AUTHORISED TO L&DT 1889 & LCT 1900
ORIGINAL SITE OF DEPOT 1903, REMOVED IN APPROX 1905
LANCASTER & D.T.Co DEPOT AT MORECAMBE
A-ORIGINAL 1889 DEPOT
B-EXTENSION BY 1911
C-RIBBLE BUS GARAGE BY 1931, DOTTED
D-OPEN FORECOURT BY 1931
LANCASTER & D.T.Co TERMINUS AT MORECAMBE
A to B TOO CLOSE FOR CARS TO PASS; DOUBLE FOR MARKET CLEARANCE ONLY
LANCASTER CORPOR'N DEPOT
ELECTRIC SIGNALS RED & GREEN IN THURNHAM ST
DEPOT BUILDING ORIGINALLY ON TOWN HALL SITE
WILLIAMSON PARK
SKERTON
BEAUMONT
TORRISHOLME
BARE
WEST END
SANDYLANDS
LOWER HEYSHAM
HIGHER HEYSHAM
HEYSHAM VILLAGE
MARSH
BOWERHAM
RIVER LUNE
L.N.W.R. TO GLASSON DOCK
L.N.W.R. TO PRESTON AND CREWE
MIDLAND RAILWAY (ELECTRIC) TO HEYSHAM HARBOUR

The ceremonial opening of the Lancaster Corporation Tramways on 14 January 1903.
(Lancaster Museum

Lancaster Corporation's depot in the 1920's. By this time the tram fleet consisted of six covered-top cars and six one-man single-deckers.
(Dr. Hugh Nicol

A single-deck raised-platform car of the Lancaster & District Tramways at the Stonewell terminus of the line to Morecambe. This line closed in 1921. *(TMS*

45

A Morecambe horse tram on the Promenade in 1924. The average service speed of the horse cars was only 4.58 miles/hr. On cold days schoolboy passengers would jump off and run alongside to keep warm.
(TMS

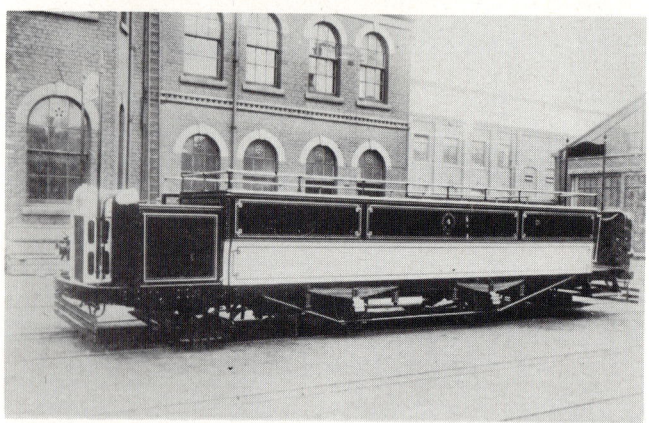

From 1912 to 1924 the tramway in Heysham was worked by four petrol trams with Leyland engines. Three were of the closed type shown on page 12, but No. 4 was an open car.
(United Electric Car Co.

Barrow-in-Furness had a steam tramway from 1885 to 1903, with Kitson engines and Falcon cars. The British Electric Traction Co. bought the company in 1899 and electrified the lines in 1903.
(TMS

47

Morecambe Corporation horse tram No. 14, built by English Electric in 1919.
(English Electric

The first electric trams in Barrow-in-Furness were operated by the British Electric Traction Co. Ltd. and included five of these bogie combination single-deckers.
(TMS

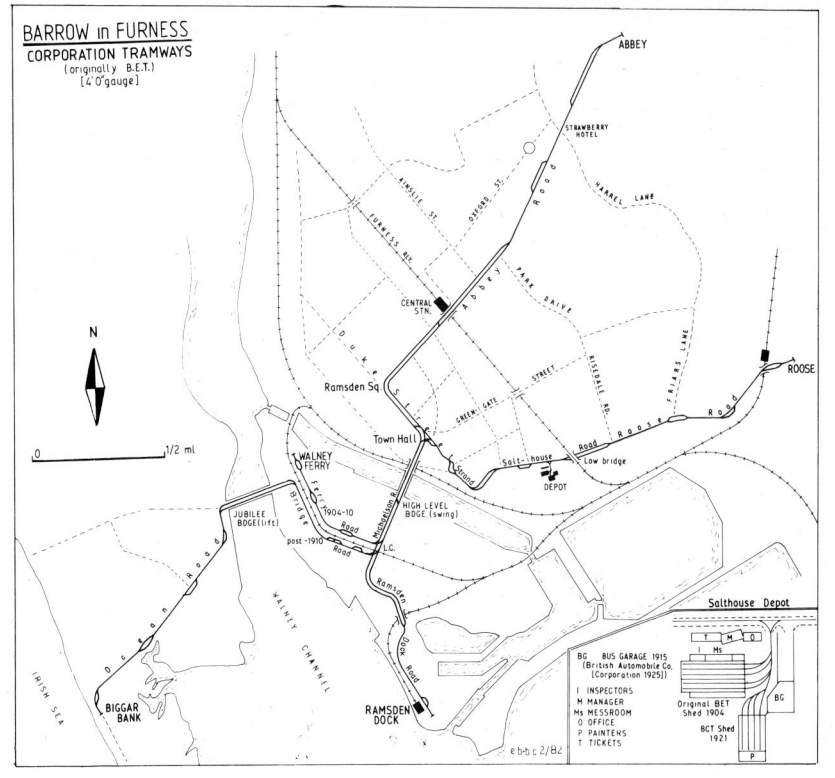

BARROW in FURNESS
CORPORATION TRAMWAYS
(originally B.E.T.)
[4'0" gauge]

BG BUS GARAGE 1915
    (British Automobile Co.
    [Corporation 1925])
I   INSPECTORS
M   MANAGER
Ms MESSROOM
O   OFFICE
P   PAINTERS
T   TICKETS

Salthouse Depot
Original BET Shed 1904
BCT Shed 1921

An original Barrow electric tram of 1903 still at work in original condition at Abbey terminus in 1929.
(Science Museum Whitcombe Collection

Barrow 17, one of four large 96-seat cars bought in 1911 for shipyard service to Walney Island.
(Science Museum Whitcombe Collection

Barrow Corporation 41, one of twelve new cars bought from Brush in 1921 to replace some of the ex-Company cars.
(Leicestershire Museums, Brush collection

CARLISLE CITY ELECTRIC TRAMWAYS
(3'6" gauge)

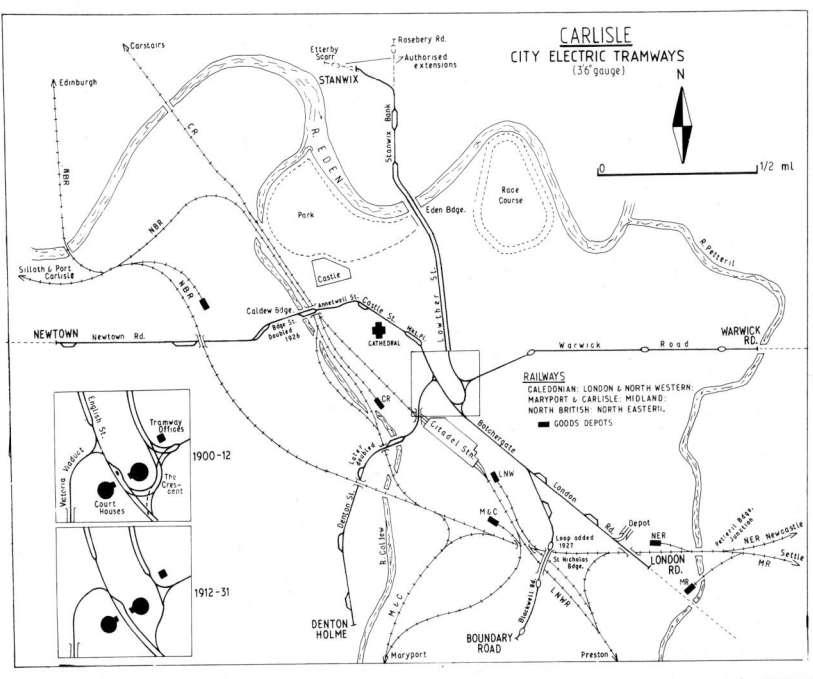

Carlisle tram No. 13 of 1900 passing the Lonsdale statue in English Street.
(Valentine & Sons)

This booklet is one of a series produced by the Light Rail Transit Association covering the history of tramways in Britain. For details, write for book list to LRTA Publications, 13A The Precinct, Broxbourne, Herts. EN10 7HY.

The original Carlisle tram fleet included three single-deckers for the Denton Holme route, which included a low bridge.
(TMS

Carlisle's original tram fleet was replaced in 1912 by 12 new cars, of which Nos. 1-8 were standard Dick, Kerr open-top vehicles.
(Dr. Hugh Nicol

Carlisle 9-12 of 1912 were Preston-built single-deckers. No. 10 is seen here on the Viaduct.
(Courtesy G. E. Baddeley

Tramcar Fleet Lists

All cars were four-wheel double-deck unless otherwise stated.
Seating figures shown thus: 22/34 are for lower and upper decks respectively.
The opening dates shown are the first day of regular public service.

Accrington Corporation Steam Tramways Company
9 miles, 4ft 0in gauge, steam traction, opened 5 April 1886, municipalised September 1907, closed 31 December 1907 (Accrington), 27 September 1908 (Haslingden).
Worked by 19 Thomas Green steam tram engines (1-9 of 1885, 10-14 of 1886, 15-16 of 1890, 17 of 1894, 18 and 6(II) of 1898). Four similar engines (19-22) were purchased in 1901 from Blackburn Corporation. There were 14 top-covered bogie trailers by Ashbury (1-9 of 1886, 10-14 of 1887) and three Milnes trailers of 1891 (15-17?). Further trailers were bought in 1899 and 1900 from Blackburn Corporation, and probably two Falcon lower saloons in 1902 from Burnley.

Accrington Corporation Tramways (electric system)
7.02 miles, 4ft 0in gauge, opened 2 August 1907, closed 6 January 1932.

Car Numbers	Type (as built)	Year Built	Builder	Seats	Truck(s)	Motors	Controllers
1-4	Single deck	1907	Brush	32	Brush Conaty (a)	Brush 2 x 40hp	Brush HD2?
5-18 (note b)	Balcony	1907	Brush	22/28	Brush Conaty (a)	Brush 2 x 40hp	Brush HD2?
5, 6(II)	Single deck	1908	Brush	32	Brush Conaty (a)	Brush 2 x 40hp	Brush HD2?
21,22	Balcony	1909	Brush	22/28	Brush Conaty (a)	Brush 2 x 40hp	Brush HD2?
23	Single deck	1909	Brush	32	Brush Conaty (a)	Brush 2 x 40hp	Brush HD2?
24,25	Balcony	1910	Brush	22/28	Brush Flexible	Brush 2 x 40hp	Brush HD2?
26	Balcony	1912	Brush	22/28	Brush Flexible	Brush 2 x 40hp	Brush HD2?
27	Single deck	1912	Brush	32	Brush Flexible	Brush 2 x 40hp	Brush HD2?
28-30 (note c)	Single deck	1915	Brush	40	Brush MET-type bogies	DK 11 2 x 40hp	DK DB1 K4
31,32 (note c)	Single deck	1920	Brush	40	Brush MET-type bogies	EE DK30B 2 x 40hp	EE DB1 K4
38,39 (note d)	Enclosed	1915	Brush	32/44?	Brush MET-type bogies	DK 11 2 x 40hp	DK DB1 K4
40,41 (note d)	Enclosed	1920	Brush	32/44?	Brush MET-type bogies	EE DK30B 2 x 40hp	EE DB1 K4
42,43 (note e)	Enclosed lowbridge	1926	Brush	26/34	Peckham P22	EE DK84 2 x 32hp	EE DB1 K44B

Notes
Livery: Bright red and cream.
(a) The Brush radial trucks were later altered to Brush Flexible type.
(b) Balcony cars 5 and 6 were renumbered 19 and 20 in 1908. Cars 9, 10 and 17 ran as open-top from 1917, but 9 and 10 received top covers again about 1928.
(c) Cars 28-32 were sold in 1932 to the Llandudno & Colwyn Bay Electric Railway, becoming L&CBER 1-5 respectively.
(d) Car 39 was sold in 1933 to Lytham St Annes Corporation for trial purposes, becoming Lytham 55. Cars 38, 40, 41 were retained for possible sale to Lytham, but were sold in 1934 to Southend-on-Sea, becoming Southend 66-68.
(e) Cars 42 and 43 were sold in 1931 to Sunderland Corporation, becoming Sunderland 19 and 20.

Barrow-in-Furness Tramways Co Ltd
5½ miles, 4ft 0in gauge, steam traction, opened 11 July 1885, closed 13 July 1903.
Operated with 8 Kitson engines and 8 Falcon double-deck cars. On 23 December 1899 the company was purchased by the British Electric Traction Co Ltd, who in 1900 added 2 Wilkinson engines and 2 cars ex North Staffordshire Tramways. Several engines and cars were destroyed by fire in June 1902, and not replaced.

BET Co Ltd and Barrow-in-Furness Corporation Tramways

In 1903 the steam tramways were electrified and operated directly by the British Electric Traction Co Ltd. Electric operation commenced 6 February 1904, transferred to Barrow-in-Furness Corporation 1 January 1920, then 6.39 miles, closed 5 April 1932.

Car Numbers	Type (as built)	Year Built	Builder	Seats	Truck(s)	Motors	Controllers
1-7	Open top	1903	Brush	22/26	Brush Type A	DK 25A 2 x 25hp	DK Form C
8-12	Single deck combination	1903	Brush	38	Brush Type B bogies	DK 25A 2 x 25hp	DK Form C
13-14	Demi car	1905	BEC	22	BEC rigid frame	Brush 800? 2 x 17hp	Raworth
15-16	Open top	1905	Brush	28/32	Brush Conaty	Brush 1002 2 x 25hp?	Brush 3A?
17-20	Open top (note a)	1911	Brush	96	Brill 22E bogies (Brush?)	Brush? 2 x 35hp	Brush 3A?
21-22	Single deck	1913	Brush	40?	Brush MET-type bogies	Brush? 2 x 35hp?	Brush 3A?
23-24	Single deck	1914	Brush	40?	Brush MET-type bogies	Brush? 2 x 35hp?	Brush 3A?
25-26	Single deck (note b)	(bought c.1915)	Midland	40	Brill 22E bogies	GE 58 2 x 35hp	BTH B18?
27-28	Open top trailer	1917	Brush	18/30	Brush	(note c)	(note c)
1-4(II) (note d)	Single deck combination	(bought 1920)	ER&TCW	32	Brill 21E	DK 25A 2 x 25hp	DK DE1 Form A
29-34 (note e)	Single deck	(bought 1920)	(note e)	28	Brill 21E	GE 52 or 58 2 x 25/35hp	BTH B6
35-46	Single deck	1921	Brush	32	Peckham P22	EE DK 29A 2 x 30hp	EE DB1 K3
—	Water car	?	Brush?	—	Brush A?	Brush?	Brush?

Livery: BET, maroon and cream; Corporation, olive green and cream.

Notes
(a) Cars 19 and 20 were converted to single deck in 1928.
(b) Built 1900 for Potteries Electric Traction Co, series 71-85.
(c) Trailers 27 and 28 were motorised after 1920, probably with trucks and equipment from 1-4.
(d) Built 1900 for Southport Corporation. 2 and 3 became works cars at Barrow.
(e) Built for Sheffield Corporation, Nos. 41 and 43 by Milnes in 1899, Nos. 100 and 102 by Brush in 1900, Nos. 126 and 206 by Sheffield Corporation in 1901 and 1902.

Blackburn Corporation Tramways Co Ltd

8¾ miles, 4ft 0in gauge, steam and horse traction, opened 28 May 1887, municipalised 24 August 1898, closed 9 August 1901. Worked by 15 Thomas Green engines of 1887/8, plus seven Beyer Peacock Wilkinson engines of 1884 bought in 1899 from the North Staffordshire Tramways Co. There were 19 bogie trailers (1-12 Ashbury 1887, 13-15 Falcon 1888, 16-19 Milnes 1889?), and eight horse trams (20-27, Milnes 1888). Some engines and cars were sold in 1901 to Accrington, and others to Rossendale. The Blackburn–Darwen route was worked separately by the Blackburn and Over Darwen Tramways Co (see next page).

Blackburn Corporation Tramways

14.73 miles, 4ft 0in gauge, opened 20 March 1899, closed 3 September 1949.

Car Numbers	Type (as built)	Year Built	Builder	Seats	Trucks	Motors	Controllers
28-35	Open top uncanopied	1899	Milnes	30/30 (note a)	Brill 22E bogies	Siemens 2 x 25hp	Siemens (note a)
36-75	Open top (note b)	1901	Milnes	32/41	Peckham 14B bogies	GE 52 6-T 4 x 20hp (note c)	BTH B6
76-81	Single deck	1907	UEC	40	Brill 22E bogies	GE 58-4T 2 x 37½hp	BTH B18
82-87	Single deck (note d)	1908	UEC	40	Brill 22E bogies	GE 58-4T 2 x 37½hp(d)	BTH B18 (note d)
88	Single deck cross bench	1908	Blackburn Corporation Tramways	46?	Brill 22E bogies	GE 58-4T 2 x 37½hp	BTH K10
No. 1	Water car/sweeper (notes e, f)	1900	Hurst Nelson	—	Brill 22E bogies	GE 58-4T 2 x 37½hp	BTH K10(2) BTH R28(1)

Blackburn Corporation Tramways *(continued)*

Livery: Dark sage green and cream.

Notes
(a) Cars 28-35 were rebuilt in 1920-23 with end canopies, then seating 30/42. Their Siemens equipments were replaced in most cases by BTH or EE equipments, except in car 29 and possibly 30 and/or 32.
(b) Cars 45, 49 and 61 received enclosed top covers in 1907, and car 62 in 1912. The remaining cars of the 36-75 class received (lower) enclosed top covers between 1923 and 1935, except for cars 36, 47, 51, 53, 54, 55, 59 and 66 which remained open-topped. The top-covered cars seated 70 (30/40), later 67 (27/40) when the lower saloons were re-seated.
(c) Car 57 received BTH 265D 35hp motors in 1926; cars 39, 43, 45, 60, 63 received BTH 265J 35hp motors ex Lanarkshire Tramways in 1932.
(d) One car (86?) was altered for one-man operation about 1920 and fitted with DK 31A 50hp motors and K3 controllers.
(e) The bogie water car was dismantled in 1908 and parts used to build cross-bench car 88.
(f) In about 1914 a permanent way towing car was made by mounting parts from the water car onto a single Brill 27G equal-wheel truck (probably ex Burnley). It was used to tow the rail wagon, salt trailers, and water tank car. The water tank trailer was also mounted onto a single Brill 27G bogie.

Blackburn and Over Darwen Tramways Company
4.93 miles, 4ft 0in, steam traction, operated by Blackburn & Over Darwen Tramways Company from 16 April 1881 to 31 December 1898 and by Darwen and Blackburn Corporations from 1 January 1899 to 16 October 1900. The first seven steam tram engines were supplied by Kitson in 1881-2; seven more came from Thomas Green between 1885 and 1896, and three Kitson engines (1, 2, 15) were purchased in 1897-8. There were 23 trailers (eight 4-wheel, eleven enclosed 8-wheel, and (briefly) four open workmen's cars in 1883. In January 1899 the stock was 13 engines and 13 cars, of which Darwen Corporation took over ten of each and Blackburn Corporation three of each.

Blackpool and Fleetwood Tramroad Company
8.21 miles, 4ft 8½in gauge, opened 14 July 1898, sold to Blackpool Corporation 1 January 1920, mostly still in use. Car numbers shown in brackets are those allocated by Blackpool Corporation in 1920.

Car Numbers	Type (as built)	Year built	Builder	Seats	Trucks	Motors	Controllers
1-10 (126-135)	Crossbench (note d)	1898	Milnes	48	Milnes bogies	GE 1000 2 x 35hp	GE K10 (note a)
11-13 (136-138)	Crossbench trailers (note b)	1898	Milnes	48	Milnes bogies (note b)	(see note b)	(see note b)
14-19 (106-111)	Single deck	1898	Milnes	48	Milnes bogies (note f)	GE 1000 2 x 35hp	GE K10 (note a)
20-24 (101-105)	Single deck	1898	Milnes	48	Milnes bogies (note f)	GE 1000 2 x 35hp	GE K10 (note a)
25-27 (139-141)	Crossbench (note e)	1899	Milnes	48	Milnes bogies	DK 44S 2 x 35hp	DK S7 (note a)
28-34 (116-122)	Single deck combination (note c)	1899	ER&TCW	55	Brill 27D bogies	DK 44S 2 x 35hp	DK S7
35-37 (123-125)	Crossbench	1910	UEC	64	UEC M&G type bogies	Westinghouse 200 2 x 35hp (note g)	Westinghouse 90M
38-41 (112-115)	Single deck (note h)	1914	UEC	48	UEC M&G type bogies	GE 67 2 x 40hp (note h)	BTH B18

Livery: Nut-brown and cream.

Notes
(a) Blackpool fitted BTH B18 controllers (probably secondhand) to cars 102-111, 123-138, 140 and 141 during the 1920s.
(b) Trailers 11-13 were motorised about 1905, with M&G swing-bolster bogies, Westinghouse 200 35hp motors and Westinghouse controllers. 137 received BTH 35hp motors in 1929. Note (a) also applies.
(c) Cars 116, 117, 119, 120 and 121 were rebuilt in 1920-21 as enclosed saloons, seating 48.
(d) Cars 126 and 132 became permanent way cars 3 and 6 about 1942. Car 127, kept as a snowplough, was restored as Blackpool & Fleetwood 2 in 1960.
(e) Car 139 was withdrawn from passenger service in 1924 and used as permanent way car and for towing rails. Car 141 was used to build an illuminated car about 1937.
(f) Cars 102-111 were retrucked with DK/M&G type bogies in 1924-26. BTH 265C 35hp motors were fitted to cars 105/9 (1925), 110 (1926), 104 (1931) and 102 (1932) and GE 200 motors to car 103 (1924).
(g) Cars 123/5 received GE 1000 motors about 1930, car 124 received BTH 265C motors in 1925.
(h) Cars 112 and 113 received BTH 265C 35hp motors about 1930-32; car 114 received BTH 509D1 40hp motors in 1928, and became works car 5 about 1942. It was restored as Blackpool & Fleetwood 40 in 1960.

Blackpool Conduit Tramway

2.9 miles, 4ft 8½in gauge, conduit current collection, opened 29 September 1885, operated by the Blackpool Electric Tramway Company Ltd until 10 September 1892, thence by Blackpool Corporation. Converted to overhead supply in summer and autumn 1899. Still operating. (Operated by horse traction 12-28 September 1885 and for short periods during 1887 and 1894, using cars 1-8 with motors removed).

Car Numbers	Type (as built)	Year built	Builder	Seats	Truck(s)	Motors	Controllers
1, 2	Open top	1885	Starbuck	56	Trunnions	Elwell Parker 1 x 7hp	Holroyd Smith
3, 4 (note d)	Open top	1885	Lancaster	16/16	Trunnions (note a)	Elwell Parker 1 x 7hp	Holroyd Smith
5, 6 (note d)	Open top	1885	Lancaster	22/22	Trunnions (note a)	Elwell Parker 1 x 7hp	Holroyd Smith
7, 8	Crossbench open top (note b)	1885	Starbuck	48	Trunnions (note b)	Elwell Parker 1 x 7hp	Holroyd Smith
9, 10	Crossbench trailer	1885	Lancaster	28	Trunnions	Elwell Parker 1 x 7hp	Holroyd Smith
9, 10(II)	Open top	1891	Milnes	56?	Trunnions	ECC	ECC
11, 12	Open top (note c)	1895	Lancaster	36/44	Equal-wheel bogies	ECC?	ECC?
13, 14	Open top (note c)	1896	Lancaster	36/44	Equal-wheel bogies	ECC?	ECC?
15, 16	Open top 'Dreadnought'	1898	Midland	36/50	Equal-wheel bogies	Siemens?	Siemens?

When the Blackpool tramway was converted from conduit to overhead supply in 1899, all sixteen cars then existing were re-equipped with two GE52 27hp motors, and GE K10 controllers. 15 and 16 received GE 54 motors and BTH 18 controllers about 1924-5.

Livery: Green and teak.

Notes
(a) Cars 3-6 were remounted in 1894 on ECC trucks (with Reckenzaun worm drive, later removed).
(b) Cars 7-8 were rebuilt in 1895 by Lancaster with closed lower decks and remounted on ECC trucks with Reckenzaun worm drive.
(c) Cars 11-14 received balcony top covers in 1915 but reverted to open top in 1924.
(d) Car 4 became a works car in 1912 and still exists, renumbered 1. Cars 5 and 6 became works cars in 1919.

Blackpool Corporation Tramways (overhead system)

11.95 miles, including 2.28 miles leased by other operators, in 1919: 19.10 miles from 1920; 20.45 from 1926; 11.15 miles in 1984. 4ft 8½in gauge. For cars of the conduit tramway operated prior to 1899, see previous list; these cars (1-16) were converted to the overhead system in 1899 but are not repeated below.

Car Numbers	Type (as built)	Year Built	Builder	Seats	Truck(s)	Motors	Controllers
17-26	Open top 'Dreadnought'	1900	Midland	44/49	Midland bogies (note o)	BTH GE52 2 x 27hp (note o)	BTH K10 (later B18)
27-41	Open top (note b)	1901	Midland	24/39	Midland (notes a, b)	BTH GE52 2 x 27hp	BTH B18
42-53	Open top (note c)	1902	Hurst Nelson	34/41	Hurst Nelson max/traction bogies (note c)	BTH GE54 2 x 28hp	BTH B18
54-61	Open top 'Dreadnought'	1902	Midland	44/49	Midland bogies	BTH GE54 2 x 28hp	BTH B18
62-64	Balcony (note d)	1911	UEC	28/38	Preston flexible	BTH GE54 2 x 28hp	BTH B18
65-67	Balcony	1911	UEC	28/36	Preston equal wheel bogies	BTH GE54 2 x 28hp	BTH B18
68	Balcony	1912	UEC	28/36		BTH GE54 2 x 28hp (note f)	BTH B18
69-70	Toastrack	1911	UEC	69 (note e)	Preston equal wheel bogies	BTH GE54? 2 x 28hp	BTH B18

Blackpool Corporation Tramways *(continued)*

Car Numbers	Type (as built)	Year Built	Builder	Seats	Truck(s)	Motors	Controllers
71-80	Toastrack	1912	UEC	69 (note e)	Preston equal wheel bogies	BTH GE52 2 x 25hp (note g)	BTH B18
81-86	Toastrack	1913	UEC				
87-92	Toastrack	1914	UEC				
93-98 (note h)	Open top	(bought 1919)	Milnes	30/42	McGuire Type 3 max/tr. bogies	Westinghouse 2 x 30hp	Westinghouse 90M
99, 100, 33-34(II)	Balcony (note m)	1923	BCT	32/46	(note j)	(note m)	(note m)
142-145	Balcony (note n)	1924/25	BCT	32/46	(note k)	BTH 265C 2 x 35hp	BTH B510
146-149	Balcony (note n)	1924	Hurst Nelson	32/46	(note k)	BTH 265C 2 x 35hp	BTH B510
150-152	Balcony (note n)	1925	Hurst Nelson	32/46	(note k)	BTH 265C 2 x 35hp	BTH B510
36, 41(II)	Balcony (note n)	1924-5	BCT	32/46	(note k)	BTH 265C 2 x 35hp	BTH B510
38-40, 42, 49(II) and 153-155	Balcony (note n)	1926	BCT	32/46	(note k)	BTH 265C 2 x 35hp	BTH B510
28, 35, 37(II) and 156-160	Balcony (note n)	1927	BCT	32/46	(note k)	BTH 265C 2 x 35hp	BTH B510
161-166 (note p)	Toastrack	1927	BCT	64 (note e)	(note k)	BTH GE52 2 x 27hp	BTH B18
45, 47, 48, 50, 53(II)	Balcony (note n)	1928	BCT	32/46	(note k)	BTH 265C 2 x 35hp	BTH B510
167-176 (note q)	Single deck	1928	EE	48 (note r)	(note k)	GEC WT28L 2 × 40hp	BTH B510
51(II), 177	Balcony (note n)	1929	BCT	32/46	(note k)	BTH 265C 2 x 35hp	BTH B510

Livery: Dark green until about 1905, then red, white and teak (green and cream from 1933-5).

Notes to cars 17-177
(a) Cars 27-41 were retrucked as follows: one car 1906 and six cars 1907 with M&G Radial, two cars 1911 with Hurst Nelson swing-bolster, two cars 1911 with Preston Flexible, three cars 1911 with Brush Flexible.
(b) Twelve cars of series 27-41 received balcony top covers in 1910-14. In 1917-19 cars 27 and 29-32 were rebuilt by BCT as balcony bogie cars on HN trucks from series 42-53, with various 35hp or 40hp motors. 30 and 31 later reverted to open-top, but received new top covers in 1928. 33 and 34 became works cars 1 and 2 about 1922. 31 became engineering car 4 in 1934.
(c) Nos. 42-53 had all received short top covers by 1915. The top covers of 42, 43, 46, 48-51 and 53 were re-used in new BCT balcony cars of the same numbers built in 1922-9.
(d) Nos. 62-64 were remounted on EE equal-wheel bogies in 1924 (62) and 1926 (63/4), with BTH 265C motors.
(e) The toastrack cars were given centre gangways in 1936-37, reducing the seating to 55 (51 for 161-6).
(f) Nos. 65-68 were re-equipped in 1920 with GE 200K 35hp motors. 65-7 later received BTH 265C motors and B510 controllers.
(g) GE54 motors in 71-6, GE52 (ex-Sheffield) in 77-92. Nos. 80, 82, 86-9 and 91-2 received BTH 265C 35hp motors in 1933-35 (bought from West Riding).
(h) Built 1901 for London United Tramways, numbers 108, 118, 125, 137, 149, 150. Retrucked at Blackpool c.1921 with 'Motherwell' type bogies built by BCT.
(j) These cars ran on HN trucks from series 42-53 until 1925-7, thence as in Note k.
(k) These cars had McGuire type equal-wheel bogies by Hurst Nelson or English Electric. HN supplied the bogies for 146-152 and parts to equip 20 other cars, EE supplied the bogies for 167-176 and sufficient bogies or parts to equip the remaining cars.
(m) BTH 265C motors and B510 controllers in 99, 100; GE 200K motors, B18 controllers in cars 33, 34.
(n) The following were later totally enclosed; 38, 39, 41, 100, 143, 155, 158-9 in 1930; 48, 49, 50 in 1938; 147, 149, 150, 160, 177 in 1940. 39 received EE bogies from car 16 in 1949.
(o) Cars 19, 20, 23, 24 and 26 had GE54 motors by 1930. Car 26 was fitted with Preston type bogies by 1930.
(p) No. 161 became salt water spray car 7 in 1944 (trailer from 1948); 163 was used to build the Blackpool Belle in 1959; 165 and 166 became television cars in 1951 and 1953 respectively (renumbered 16, 17 in 1968). 166 was restored to original 1927 state at Crich in 1973.
(q) 168-175 were retrucked in 1950 with English Electric bogies from cars 10-21 of 1939. 167 became a permanent way car in 1954 (with BTH 265C motors) and is now preserved; 168 became the Rocket illuminated car in 1961; 174 became the Santa Fe trailer in 1962; 170 was a permanent way car in 1962-5 and was then used to build HMS Blackpool.
(r) Plus two seats on each platform, probably only for use at the rear end.

General note: There were many changes of equipment to individual cars in the 1920s and early 1930s, additional to those listed above.

Blackpool Corporation Tramways (contd). Modern fleet prior to 1968 renumbering.

In this list the term 'railcoach' denotes a streamlined centre-entrance single-decker, 'boat' denotes a modern-style open centre-entrance single-deck car, and 'sun saloon' denotes a railcoach with part-open sides and opening roof. All cars have equal-wheel bogies.

Car Numbers	Type (as built)	Year built	Builder	Seats	Trucks	Motors	Controllers
200	Railcoach	1933	EE	48 (note a)	EE bogies	EE 305A 2 × 57hp	EE DB1 Z4
201-224	Railcoach	1933/4	EE	48 (note a)	EE bogies (note h)	EE 305A 2 × 57hp	EE DB1 Z4
225	'Boat' (low sides)	1934	EE	56	EE bogies	EE DK34(b) 2 × 37hp	EE DB1 K44E (note c)
226-236	'Boat'	1935	EE	56	EE bogies	EE 327A 2 × 40hp	BTH B18 (notes b, c)
237 (note d)	Open top c/entrance(d)	1934	EE	40/54	EE bogies	EE 305E(q) 2 × 57hp	EE DB1 K44
238-249	Open top c/entrance(d)	1934	EE	40/54	EE bogies	EE 305E 2 × 57hp	EE DB1 Z6
250-263	Double deck c/entrance	1934/5	EE	40/44 (note e)	EE bogies	EE 305E 2 × 57hp	EE DB1 Z6
264-283	Railcoach (note f)	1935	EE	48 (note f)	EE bogies	EE 305E 2 × 57hp	EE DB1 Z6
284-303	Railcoach (Brush type)	1937	Brush	48 (note a)	EMB bogies (note h)	CP C162 2 × 57hp(g)	Allen West (note g)
10-21	Sun saloon (note j)	1939	EE	56 (note j)	EE bogies (note h)	BTH 265C 2 × 35hp (notes b, h)	EE DB1 K53E (note h)
304-328	Single deck c/entrance	1952-3 (note k)	Roberts	56	M&T HS44 bogies	CP C92 4 × 45hp	CP Vambac (note m)
T1-10	Single deck c/entrance trailers	1960-1 (note n)	MCW	66 (note p)	M&T bogies	—	(note p)

Livery: Green and cream, various styles (mostly green c.1933-57, later mostly cream).

Notes
(a) Plus two folding seats in centre vestibule (later removed).
(b) Equipment transferred from older Blackpool cars and modified by EE.
(c) 225, 226 and 236 received EE K53E controllers from 10-21 series in 1951 (236 in 1959).
(d) 237-249 were top-covered in 1941/2. 237 was delivered as 226 and renumbered later in 1934.
(e) 253, 255, 256 re-seated to 40/54 in 1960-61, also 258 in 1967.
(f) 272-282 were fitted for trailer haulage in 1960-61. 272-7 and 281 were semi-permanently coupled to trailers T1-7 from 1963/4 and seated 53, with one set of controls removed.
(g) Re-equipped 1963-7 with EE 305A motors and EE Z4 controllers from 200-224 class cars.
(h) 208, 303 and 10-21 received M&T HS44 bogies, CP C92 4 × 45hp motors and CP Vambac control in 1949-52 (208 and 303 in 1946-7).
(j) Enclosed in 1942, re-seated to 48 in 1948-51.
(k) 304-10 delivered 1952, remainder 1953.
(m) Replaced by EE Z4 controllers from 1964 on cars 306/10/18/19 and 321-8.
(n) T1-8 delivered 1960, T9-10 in 1961.
(p) T1-7 fitted with one Z6 controller in 1963/4 and seating reduced to 61, to run semi-permanently with 281 and 272-7.
(q) As delivered in 1934 this car had EE DK34B 37hp motors.

Blackpool Corporation Tramways (contd). 1968 Fleet Renumbering.

Car Numbers	Former Numbers	Type	Year Built	Builder	Seats	Trucks	Motors	Controllers
600	225	Boat (low sides)	1934	EE	56	EE	EE 327A 2 × 40hp	EE DB1 K44E
601-7	226-8, 230, 233/5/6	Boat	1934	EE	56	EE	EE 327A(k) 2 × 40hp	BTH B18(a)
610 (note b)	224	Railcoach	1934	EE	48	EE	EE 305A 2 × 57hp	EE DB1 Z4
611-620 (notes b, c)	264-271, 282/3	Railcoach	1935	EE	48	EE	EE 305E 2 × 57hp	EE DB1 Z6
621-638 (note e)	284-300, 302	Brush Railcoach	1937	Brush	48	EMB	EE 305(d) 2 × 57hp	EE DB1 Z4 (note f)
660(m)	324	Coronation	1953	Roberts	56	M&T HS44	CP C92 4 × 45hp	EE DB1 Z4
641	—	New single deck car	1984	East Lancs.	54	BCT	EE 305 2 × 57hp	Brush thyristor

Blackpool Corporation Tramways *(continued)* 1968 Fleet Renumbering

Car Numbers	Former Numbers	Type	Year Built	Builder	Seats	Trucks	Motors	Controllers
671-677	281, 272-277	Twin car motors	1935	EE	53	EE	EE 305E 2 x 57hp	EE DB1 Z6
678-680	278-280	Twin car motors	1935	EE	48	EE	EE 305E 2 x 57hp	EE DB1 Z6
681-687	T1-7	Trailers	1960	MCW	61	M&T	—	EE DB1 Z6
688-690	T8-10	Trailers	1960-1	MCW	66	M&T	—	—
700-712	237-249	Double deck	1934	EE	40/54	EE	EE 305 2 x 57hp	EE DB1 Z6
713-726 (note g)	250-263	Double deck	1934/5	EE	40/54 (note h)	EE	EE 305 2 x 57hp	EE DB1 Z6
761	—	Double deck	1979	BCT	42/56	EE	EE 305hp 2 × 57hp	Westinghouse thyristor
762	—	Double deck	1982	BCT	34/56	BCT	EE 305 2 × 57hp	Brush thyristor

Livery: Cream with green trim. One-man cars 1-13 (note b) were crimson and yellow until 1975-7, then red and cream; 761/2 (note g) are dark green and cream.

Notes
(a) EE DB1 K53E controllers in 607. EE DB1 K44E controllers in 601 to 1971 and 606 from 1971.
(b) Reconstructed by BCT as 48-seat one-man cars 1-13 (former numbers 616, 620, 610, 609, 608, 617, 619, 612, 613, 614, 615, 611, 618) in 1972 (1-5), 1973 (6, 7), 1974 (8, 9), 1975 (10-12) and 1976 (13). Z4 controllers. The numbers 608 and 609 had not yet been carried by 220 or 221 when withdrawn for rebuilding.
(c) 618 was lengthened by BCT in 1968 to seat 56.
(d) EE 327A 40hp motors in car 622 (used as permanent way car), still with Allen West CTJ controllers.
(e) 638 was rebuilt as prototype one-man car in 1969, with Crompton West controllers.
(f) Z6 controllers in 623/4/7, 631/3/4.
(g) 725 reconstructed by BCT 1979 as 98-seat one-man double deck car 761 with Westinghouse 'chopper' control; 714 reconstructed similarly in 1982 as 762, but with 90 seats and Brush control.
(h) Four cars reseated from 40/44 to 40/54 (717, 720 in 1978, 715, 722 in 1979).
(j) 689 and 690 sold to GEC Traction Ltd in 1982.
(k) DK 34B 27hp motors in car 601.
(m) 660 is the sole survivor at Blackpool of Coronation cars 304-328 of 1952/3, of which 304-312 and 314-328 were renumbered 641-664 in 1968 but were withdrawn by 1970.

General note: The Z6 controllers had four series, three parallel and one field shunt notch. From 1960 onwards they were altered to four series and four parallel notches, and thus became the same as Z4.

Blackpool Corporation Tramways. Illuminated Cars.

Car	Former Number	1968 Number	First Season	Final Season	Seats	Truck(s)	Motors	Controllers
Double deck 68	—	—	1912	1938	78	DK bogies	GE 200K 2 x 40hp	BTH B18
Lifeboat	40	—	1926	1961	20	Brush Flexible	GE 52 2 x 27hp	GE K10
Gondola	28	—	1927	1962	20	Brush? AA	GE 52 2 x 27hp	GE K10
'Progress' (note a)	141	—	1949	1958	—	Milnes bogies	GE 1000 2 x 35hp(c)	BTH B18
Double deck 158, 159	—	—	1959	1966	78	DK bogies	BTH 265 2 x 40hp	BTH B510
Blackpool Belle	163	731	1959	1978	32	DK bogies	GE 52 2 x 27hp	BTH B18
Rocket	168	732	1961	in use	47	EE bogies	GEC WT28L 2 x 50hp	(note b)
Western Train engine	209	733	1962	in use	35	EE bogies	EE 305 2 x 57hp	(note b)
Western Train coach	174	734	1962	in use	60	EE bogies	—	Allen West (one only)
Hovertram	222	735	1963	in use	99	EE bogies	EE 305 2 x 57hp	(note b)
HMS Blackpool	170	736	1965	in use	66	EE bogies	GEC WT28L 2 x 50hp	(note b)

Notes
(a) Rebuilt from 1937 decorated car (ex-141).
(b) Each car has one EE Z4 or K53E controller at the leading end and one Allen West controller at the trailing end (733/4 are one two-car unit).
(c) Later replaced by GE 52 25hp motors.

Blackpool Corporation Tramways. Engineering Cars.
(excluding passenger cars used for works purposes without being renumbered).

Car	Former Number	Later Number	First year In use	Last year In use	Truck(s)	Motors	Controllers
Overhead line car (ex conduit)	4	4(b)	1912	1934?	ECC	GE 52 2 x 27hp	BTH GE K10
Engineering car 2	33	—	1920?	1928?	Brush flexible	GE 200K 2 x 40hp	BTH B18
Grinder/ snowplough 1 (2 from 1968 to 1972)	—	752(a)	1924	in use	MSCC	GE 200K 2 x 40hp	BTH B18
Electric locomotive (works number 717)	—	—	1927	1963	EE rigid frame	EE DK30/1M 2 x 50hp	EE DB1 K44C
Grinder/ snowplough 2	—	—	1928	1965	Brush flexible	GE 200K 2 x 40hp	BTH B18
Overhead line car 4	31	754(a)	1934	in use	DK bogies	BTH 265 2 x 35hp	BTH B510
Permanent way car 5 (Fleetwood box)	114	—	1936	1960	DK bogies	BTH 509D1 2 x 40hp	BTH B510
Permanent way car 3 (cross-bench)	126	—	1939	1951	Milnes bogies	GE 1000 2 x 35hp	BTH B18
Permanent way car 6 (cross-bench)	132	—	1939	1955	Milnes bogies	GE 1000 2 x 35hp	BTH B18
Salt water spray 7 (trailer from 1948)	161	—	1942	1958	DK bogies	BTH 265C 2 x 35hp(c)	BTH B18(c)
Television car	165	16	1951	1968	DK bogies	GE 52 2 x 27hp	BTH B18
Television car	166	17	1951	1971	DK bogies	GE 52 2 x 27hp	BTH B18
Diesel-electric overhead line car 3	143	753(a)	1958	in use	DK bogies	BTH 265C 2 x 35hp	BTH B510
Permanent way car 5	221	—	1965	1971	EE bogies	CP C162 2 x 57hp	Allen West CTJ
PW flat car with hydraulic crane	628	751	1973	in use	EMB bogies	—	—

Also trailers 749 (tower wagon) and 750 (reel wagon) acquired from Blackpool & Fleetwood Tramroad in 1920.

Livery: Most engineering cars have been in all-over green livery.

Notes
(a) The numbers 749-754 were allocated in 1972.
(b) Renumbered incorrectly as 1 on restoration in 1960.
(c) Electrical equipment removed in 1948.

These two former Blackpool and Fleetwood cross-bench cars survived until 1951/2, No. 128 as a snow plough and No. 3 (ex-126) as a permanent way car.

(J. Copland)

Burnley & District Tramways Co Ltd

7.01 miles, 4ft 8½in gauge, opened 17 September 1881, municipalised 1 March 1900, closed 17 November 1901. Worked by 5 Kitson engines (1-5 of 1881) and 12 Falcon engines (6-9 of 1883, 10 of 1884, 11-13 of 1885, 14 of 1889, 15 of 1896, 16-17 of 1897). Trailer cars: 1-7 Starbuck 4-wheel 1881 (originally top-covered), 8-10 Starbuck 8-wheel 1884, 11-12, 3(ii), 6(ii) Starbuck 1885, 13 Falcon 1888, 14-15 Falcon 1897, 16 Metropolitan bought 1900 from St. Helens. The 1881 locomotives were withdrawn from 1 May 1882, and horse traction used until improved locomotives were delivered in March, 1883.

Burnley Corporation Tramways

13.05 miles (including 2.70 miles leased), 4ft 0in gauge, opened 16 December 1901, closed 7 May 1935.

Car Numbers	Type (as built)	Year Built	Builder	Seats	Truck(s)	Motors	Controllers
1-24 (note a)	Open top (note b)	1901-2	Milnes	32/39	Brill 22E (note d)	GE 58-4T 2 x 37½hp	BTH B18
25-38	Open top (notes b, c)	1903	Milnes	32/39	Brill 22E (note d)	GE 58-4T 2 x 37½hp	BTH B18
39-46	Single deck	1903	ER&TCW	44	Brill 27G bogies (note d)	DK 25B 4 x 25hp	DK QB1A
47	Single deck	1907	UEC	40	Simpson & Park pivotal (note e)	GE 58-4T 2 x 37½hp	BTH B18
48-52	Balcony	1909	Hurst Nelson	32/39	Brill 22E bogies (note d)	GE 58-4T 2 x 37½hp	BTH B18
53-54	Single deck	1910	UEC	44	Burnley m/tr bogies (note f)	GE 58-4T 2 x 37½hp	BTH B18
55-57	Single deck	1911	UEC	44			
58-67	Balcony	1913	UEC	32/39	Burnley m/tr bogies (note f)	GE 58-4T 2 x 37½hp	BTH B18
68-72 (note g)	Single deck	1921	EE	44	Burnley m/tr bogies (note f)	GE 58-4T 2 x 37½hp	BTH B18
1	Water car (note h)	1903	Burnley Corpn. Trys.	—	rigid frame	GE 58-4T 2 x 37½hp	BTH B18
2	Water car (note h)	1925	Burnley Corpn. Trys.	—	rigid frame	GE 58-4T 2 x 37½hp	BTH B18

There were also three goods wagons, one welding trailer, and one bogie rail-carrying wagon.

Livery: Chocolate and primrose.

Notes
(a) Car 10 was renumbered 68 in 1926 following accident damage.
(b) Cars 9-11 received Hurst Nelson balcony top covers in 1910; cars 1-8 and 12-38 received balcony top covers in 1911-20 (14 by UEC, 21 by Burnley). The top-covered cars seated 30/43.
(c) Cars 25-38 were built with top-deck windshields and retained these until top-covered. One car of series 1-24 was fitted similarly.
(d) The Brill 27G bogies were replaced in 1914 by 'Burnley' bogies with GE58 motors (and B18 Controllers). The Brill 22E bogies of cars 1-38 were dismantled and rebuilt with new parts to produce Burnley bogies, referred by Burnley as Type C trucks.
(e) The Simpson & Park pivotal trucks were altered by Burnley to maximum-traction trucks (by adding pony wheels). These 'Burnley' bogies were subsequently made by several manufacturers.
(f) The new Burnley bogies were made by Mountain & Gibson and UEC, as well as by Burnley Corporation Tramways.
(g) Single-deck car 68 was renumbered 73 in 1926.
(h) The two water cars resembled centre-cab locomotives and could also be used for snow sweeping and rail grinding, and for hauling goods wagons. The Corporation classified them as locomotives.

After the formation of the Burnley, Colne, and Nelson Joint Transport Committee on 1 April 1933, the Burnley trams were given a suffix B to their numbers.

For regular news and articles on tramways and light railways read *Modern Tramway*, published monthly be the Light Rail Transit Association. Trade publication by Ian Allan Ltd.

City of Carlisle Electric Tramways Co Ltd
5.73 miles, 3ft 6in gauge, opened 30 June 1900, closed 21 November 1931.

Car Numbers	Type (as built)	Year Built	Builder	Seats	Truck	Motors	Controllers
1-3	Single deck	1900	ER&TCW	22	Brill 21E	Walker 33N 2 x 25hp	DK S7
4-15	Open top (note a)	1900	ER&TCW	22/23	Brill 21E	Walker 33N 2 x 25hp	DK S7
1-8(II)	Double deck	1912	UEC	22/28	Brill 21E	GE 58 (ex-MET) 2 x 28hp	BTH K10D
9-12(II)	Single deck	1912	UEC	24	Brill 21E	GE 58 (ex-MET) 2 x 28hp	BTH K10D
13(II) (note b)	Open top	(bought 1920)?	ER&TCW	22/26	Brill 21E	DK 25B? 2 x 25hp	DK DB1 Form B
15(II) (note d)	Open top	1923	EE	22/26	Brill 21E	Westinghouse 46M 2 x 25hp	Westinghouse 210
14(II) (note c)	Open top	1925	EE	22/26	Brill 21E	DK 25B? 2 x 25hp	DK DB1 Form B

Livery: Chocolate and cream to 1912, then dark green and cream.

Notes
(a) Car 14 is thought to have been rebuilt as a works car about 1910.
(b) Car 13(II) is thought to have been a former Ilkeston Corporation tram of series 1-8.
(c) Car 14(II) was a new EE body for an existing truck, probably ex-Ilkeston series 1-8.
(d) Car 15(II) was a new EE body for an existing truck, probably ex-Ilkeston series 9-13.
One car received DK 29A 30hp motors and DK K33B controllers in 1928.

Colne and Trawden Light Railway Company, and Colne Corporation
5.23 miles, 4ft 0in gauge, opened 30 November 1903, taken over by Colne Corporation 25 March 1914, and by Burnley Colne and Nelson Joint Transport Committee 1 April 1933, closed 6 January 1934.

Car Numbers	Type (as built)	Year Built	Builder	Seats	Truck(s)	Motors	Controllers
1-6	Open top (note a)	1903	Milnes	22/28	Milnes (note b)	GE 58-6T 2 x 28hp	BTH B18
7-10	Open top (note a)	1905	Brush	22/26	Brush Conaty(b)	GE 58-6T 2 x 28hp	BTH B18
11-12	Open top (note a)	1906	Milnes Voss	22/28	M&G 21EM	GE 58-6T 2 x 28hp	BTH B18
13	Balcony	1914	UEC	52	Preston flexible?	GE 58-4T 2 x 37½hp	BTH B18
2-3(II)	Balcony	1921	EE	68	EE Burnley bogies	GE 58-4T 2 x 37½hp	BTH B18
14-16	Enclosed	1926	Brush	52	Peckham P22	MV 101BR 2 x 40hp	MV OK6B

Livery: Royal blue and white to about 1922, Maroon and cream from about 1923.

Notes
(a) Cars 1-6 received Milnes Voss balcony top covers in 1911, and two of these cars were rebuilt as 20-seat one-man single-deck cars in 1924-5. Three other open top cars were rebuilt as balcony cars by UEC in 1915. The top-covered cars seated 52.
(b) The Milnes trucks were replaced by Preston or Brush 21E trucks from 1914 onwards; the Brush truck of car 8 was altered in 1914 to P22 type. Other trucks were converted similarly, and two new P22 trucks were bought from Brush in 1926. A Peckham R24 radial truck was tried in 1914.
(c) After the formation of the Joint Committee in 1933 the ten remaining Colne trams were given a suffix C to their numbers.

Preston horse tramways (continued from page 63)
Preston Tramways Company
2.45 miles (Town Hall—Fulwood), 3ft 6in gauge, horse operated, opened 20 March 1879, operation transferred 1 January 1887 to Messrs. W. Harding & Co, worked by six double-deck cars, closed 31 December 1903.

Preston Corporation Tramways (W. Harding & Co Ltd)
4.56 miles (Fishergate Hill to Farringdon Park and Ashton), 3ft 6in gauge, horse operated, opened 14 April 1882, leased to W. Harding & Co Ltd, worked by 8 double-deck cars, closed 31 December 1903.

Darwen Corporation Tramways
4.36 miles, 4ft 0in gauge, opened 17 October 1900, closed 5 October 1946.

Car Numbers	Type (as built)	Year Built	Builder	Seats	Truck(s)	Motors	Controllers
1-5	Open top	1900	Milnes	30/42	Brill 22E bogies	Westinghouse 2 x 30hp?	Westinghouse
6-10	Open top	1900	Milnes	30/42	Brill 22E bogies	GE 52-4T 2 x 25hp	BTH B18
11-14	Open top (note a)	1901	Milnes	60	Brill 21E	GE 58-4T 2 x 37½hp	BTH B18
15	Demi car (note b)	1905	Milnes Voss	22	M&G 21EM	Westinghouse 2 x ?hp	Raworth-Westinghouse
16-17	Demi car	1906	Milnes Voss	22	M&G 21EM	Westinghouse 2 x ?hp	Raworth-Westinghouse
18-19	Open top	1915	UEC	30/36	Peckham P25 bogies	DK 20A 2 x 40hp	DK DB1 K3
20-22	Open top	1921	EE	30/36	EE Burnley bogies	DK 20A2 2 x 40hp	DK DB1 K3
16-17(II)	Enclosed	1924	Brush	30/42	Burnley bogies	BTH 502AS 2 x 42hp	BTH B510
3, 5, 7, 8, 15(II)	Enclosed	1925-9	DCT (note c)	30/42	Burnley bogies	BTH 502AS 2 x 42hp	BTH B18
10(ii)	Enclosed	1933	DCT (note d)	30/42	Burnley bogies	? MV	BTH B510M
9(II)	Enclosed	Bought 1933	(note e)	?			
11(II)	Balcony	Bought 1933	(note e)	?			
23, 24 (note f)	Enclosed centre-entrance	1936	EE	24/32	EE max/ traction bogies	EE 305A 2 x 57hp	EE K33E (note f)

Livery: Vermillion and purple lake, later vermillion and cream.

Notes
(a) Car 13 received a Milnes Voss Magrini top cover in 1903; car 14 received a balcony top ex-Accrington in 1919.
(b) Demi-car 15 became works car No. 1 in 1912.
(c) New cars 3, 5, 7, 8, 15 were reconstructed lower saloons with new Brush top covers (No. 15's saloon was from original No. 1).
(d) New car 10 was a lower saloon reconstructed by DCT with a top cover ex-Rawtenstall.
(e) Cars 9(ii) and 11(II) were ex-Rawtenstall, but 11 was placed on the truck of the former Darwen 11.
(f) 23 and 24 became Llandudno & Colwyn Bay 24 and 23 in 1946. 23's controllers are now on Seaton 12.
(g) In 1941 a new car 10 was made from the lower deck of 17 and top deck of 8, after 17 had overturned and 8 and 10 had been withdrawn.

Haslingden Corporation Tramways
2.90 miles, 4ft gauge, purchased 1 January 1908 from Accrington Corporation Steam Tramways Company and worked by eight Thomas Green steam engines and seven cars purchased from Accrington. Electric operation commenced 5 September 1908, with cars supplied by Accrington, but Haslingden Corporation retained one steam tram engine and one wagon for permanent way work and snow clearing. Closed 30 April 1930.

Lancaster Corporation Tramways
2.99 miles, 4ft 8½in gauge, opened 14 January 1903, closed 31 March 1930.

Car Numbers	Type (as built)	Year Built	Builder	Seats	Truck(s)	Motors	Controllers
1-10	Open top (note a)	1902	Lancaster (note b)	18/23	Brill 21	Westinghouse 2 x 25hp	Westinghouse
11-12	Open top (note a)	1905	Milnes Voss	18/23	M&G 21EM	Westinghouse 2 x 25hp	Westinghouse

Livery: Chocolate and primrose.

Notes
(a) Six cars received balcony top covers (four by Milnes Voss 1911, two by UEC 1913, then seating 18/24. The remaining six open-top cars were converted in 1917-23 to one-man single-deck cars (nos. 1, 10, 11, 12 and two of 4, 5, 7), seating 24.
(b) In April 1902 the Lancaster Railway Carriage & Wagon Co Ltd was absorbed by the Metropolitan Amalgamated Railway Carriage and Wagon Co Ltd.

Lancaster and District Tramways Company

4.30 miles, 4ft 8½in gauge, horse traction, opened 2 August 1890, closed 31 December 1921. Worked by 14 double-deck cars built by Lancaster in 1890, seating 18/22, of which some were later altered to single-deck open cars by lowering the top deck to car waist level.

Lytham St Annes Corporation Tramways (and predecessor companies).

6.31 miles, 4ft 8½in gauge. Opened 11 July 1896 with gas trams by the British Gas Traction Co Ltd, sold in 1898 to the Blackpool, St Annes and Lytham Tramways Co Ltd, electric traction commenced 28 May 1903, acquired 28 October 1920 by St Annes UDC (Lytham St Annes Corporation from 1922), closed 28 April 1937. An additional 1.20 miles was leased from Blackpool until 1917; this section was horse-operated in 1900-2. Of the 16 gas trams, Nos. 1-4 seated 40, Nos. 5-16 seated 52.

Car Numbers	Type (as built)	Year Built	Builder	Seats	Truck(s)	Motors	Controllers
1-20	Open top	1903	BEC	22/32 (note a)	BEC SB60 (note a)	GE 52-4T 2 x 25hp	BTH B18
21-30	Open top (note b)	1903	BEC	22/32	BEC SB60	GE 52-4T 2 x 25hp	BTH B18
31-40	Open top/ crossbench	1905	Brush	34/34	Brush Conaty	GE 52-4T 2 x 25hp	BTH B18
41-50	Balcony	1924	EE	23/38	Peckham P22	EE DK 84B 2 x 32hp	EE DB1 K3
51-54 (note c)	Single deck	(bought 1933)	EE	36	Peckham P22	EE DK 30B 2 x 40hp	EE DB1 K3
55 (note d)	Enclosed	(bought 1933)	Brush	32/44?	Brush MET-type bogies	DK 11 2 x 40hp	DK DB1 K4
56 (note e)	Enclosed	(bought 1934)	(note e)	22/40	Preston standard	EE DK 94 2 x 32hp	DK DB1 C Special

Livery: Bright blue and cream.

Notes
(a) Cars 6, 9, 11 reseated 20/32 in 1927-8 (car 6 remounted on Brush 21E truck).
(b) Rebuilt by UEC 1906 with cross-bench lower decks to seat 28/32. 26 became sweeper/grinder in 1930.
(c) Built in 1924 for the Dearne District Light Railway (series 1-25).
(d) Built 1915 for Accrington Corporation (car 39).
(e) Built 1928 or 1929 by Preston Corporation (car 42).

Morecambe Tramways Company

2.77 miles, 4ft 8½in gauge, horse traction, opened 3 June 1887, 1.58 miles sold to Morecambe Corporation 20 July 1909, remainder worked by petrol cars from 5 January 1912, closed 24 October 1924.

Car Numbers	Type (as built)	Year Built	Builder	Seats	Truck	Motors	Controllers
1, 2	Open top	1887	Lancaster	20/24	—	—	—
3, 4	Toastrack	1887	Lancaster	28?	—	—	—
5, 6	Open top	1888	Lancaster	20/24	—	—	—
7	Open top	1889	Lancaster	20/24	—	—	—
8-11	Open top	1897	Lancaster	20/24	—	—	—
12-15	Open top (note a)	(bought c.1898)	?	?	—	—	—
16, 17	Open top (note a)	(bought 1901)	?	?	—	—	—

Fourteen cars were sold to Morecambe Corporation in 1909. Three cars were retained by the company until 1913 and were then transferred to the Corporation.

| 1-3(II) | Single deck petrol cars | 1911 | Leyland/ UEC | 35(b) | UEC | Leyland 55hp engine | — |
| 4(II) | Open petrol car | 1913 | Leyland UEC | 35(b) | UEC | Leyland 55hp engine | — |

Livery: Maroon, teak and white, later green, some cars maroon and white.

Notes
(a) Horse cars 12-15 were smaller than 1-2 and 5-11, and may have been second-hand (source unknown). Two more cars were bought in 1901, details not known.
(b) Plus two platform seats.

Morecambe Corporation Tramways

2.38 miles, 4ft 8½in gauge, horse traction, commenced operating 20 July 1909, closed 6 October 1926. The Corporation took over Morecambe Tramways Company cars 1-14, and bought four replacement horse cars from English Electric, 13, 14 in 1919 and 15, 16 in 1922. 13 and 16 were double-deck, seating 18/22?; 14 and 15 were single-deck toastrack, seating 32. Car 1 of 1887 was sold in 1926 to Manchester Corporation for use in an anniversary parade.

Nelson Corporation Tramways

2.75 miles (plus 0.76 miles leased to Burnley). 4ft 0in gauge, opened 23 February 1903, merged with Burnley and Colne to form BCN Joint Committee 1 April 1933, closed 6 January 1934.

Car Numbers	Type (as built)	Year Built	Builder	Seats	Truck(s)	Motors	Controllers
1-3	Open top (note a)	1902	Brush	40	Brush A	GE 58-6T 2 x 28hp	BTH B18
4-6	Open top	1903	Brush	40	Brush A	GE 58-6T 2 x 28hp	BTH B18
7, 8	Single deck combination	1903	ER&TCW	38 bogies	Brill 22E 2 x 25hp	DK 25B	DK Form C
9	Single deck combination	1904	ER&TCW	38	Brill 22E bogies	DK 25B 2 x 25hp	DK Form C
10, 11	Balcony (note c)	1912	UEC	55	Preston flexible?	Siemens 2 x 40hp	Siemens
12	Water car/ sweeper	1905	UEC	—	Brill 21E	DK 25B 2 x 25hp	DK DB1 Form C
1-6(II)	Balcony (note c)	1916	UEC	55	Preston standard?	(note b)	BTH B18
7-9(II)	Balcony (note c)	1925	Brush	55	Brush 21E	MV 104 2 x 50hp	MV T1/D

Livery: Red and white, later brown and cream.

Notes
(a) Car 3 received a Milnes Voss Magrini top cover in 1903, which was later removed.
(b) Cars 1-6(II) probably used the GE 58 motors from original 1-6.
(c) These cars were of lowbridge design.

The section of line leased to Burnley was operated by the Burnley & District Tramways Company with steam trams from 17 September 1881 to 21 November 1901, and by Burnley Corporation electric cars from 26 March 1902.

After the formation of the Joint Committee on 1 April 1933, the Nelson trams were given a suffix N to their fleet numbers.

Preston horse tramways (see page 60)

Preston Corporation Tramways (electric)

10.53 miles, 4ft 8½in gauge, opened 7 June 1904, closed 15 December 1935.

Car Numbers	Type (as built)	Year Built	Builder	Seats	Truck(s)	Motors	Controllers
1-26	Open top (note a)	1904	ER&TCW	22/26	Brill 21E	DK 25A 2 x 25hp	DK Form C Special
27-30	Open top	1904	ER&TCW	30/38	Brill 22E bogies	DK 3A4 2 x 35hp	DK Form C Special
31-33	Single deck	1912	UEC	40	Brill 39E bogies	DK 9A3 2 x 40hp	DK DB1 K3
34-39	Balcony (note b)	1914	UEC	22/30	Preston flexible	DK 9A3 2 x 40hp	DK DB1 K3
40-45	Single deck	(bought 1918)	(note c)	28	Brill 21E	DK 25A 2 x 25hp	DK DB1 Form D
46-48 (note d)	Single deck	(bought 1920)	(note d)	28	Brill 21E	DK 25A 2 x 25hp	DK DB1 Form D
30, 40, 42 (II)	Enclosed	1928-9	Preston Corporation	22/40	Preston standard	EE DK94 2 x 32hp	DK Form C Special
13, 18, 22 (II)	Balcony	(bought 1929 (note e)	EE	22/30	Preston standard	EE DK 30B 2 x 40hp	DK DB1 K4

Livery: Dark red and cream.

Notes
(a) Ten cars were fitted with UEC short top covers in 1907, five more in 1908, three more in 1913. About nine cars were enclosed in 1924-28 and received DK 94 32hp motors, probable numbers 1, 3, 5, 6, 9, 17, 19, 23, 24. All or most of these cars were re-seated to 16/26.
(b) Two cars (35, 38) were all-enclosed from about 1928, and re-seated to 16/38.
(c) Built for Sheffield Corporation, Nos. 125 and 129 by Sheffield Corporation in 1901, 187 and 188 by Milnes in 1902, 207 and 209 by Sheffield Corporation in 1903. Their BTH equipments were replaced at Preston by Dick Kerr equipments bought by Sheffield from the LCC Tramways but sent direct to Preston.
(d) Built in 1900 by Brush for Sheffield Corporation, Nos. 89, 90 and 95. Re-equipped at Preston as for cars 40-45. Car 48 was renumbered 12 in 1929.
(e) Built 1919 for City of Lincoln Tramways, Lincoln numbers 9, 10, 11.

Car 42 was sold in 1934 to Lytham St Annes Corporation, becoming Lytham 56.

Rossendale Valley Tramways Company

6.35 miles, 4ft gauge, opened 31 January 1889, steam traction. Worked by Thomas Green engines 1-9 (1888-9), 10 (1893), 11 (1894) and 12 (ex-Blackburn in 1901), with double-deck cars 1-10 (Milnes, 1889), 11 (ex-Blackburn in 1901) and 12 (ex-Blackburn ? in 1903). Purchased 1 October 1908 by Rawtenstall and Bacup Corporations. Closed 22 July 1909. Two steam tram engines were retained by Rawtenstall as snowploughs.

Rawtenstall Corporation Tramways

11.75 miles, 4ft gauge, opened 15 May 1909, closed 31 March 1932. (Ceremonial closure on 7 April.)

Car Numbers	Type (as built)	Year Built	Builder	Seats	Truck(s)	Motors	Controllers
1-16	Balcony (note a)	1909	UEC	22/29	Preston 21E	Westinghouse 220	Westinghouse T1/R (Raworth) (note b)
17, 18	Balcony	1912	UEC	22/28	Brill 21E	Siemens?	Siemens?
19-24	Single deck	1912	UEC	30 (note c)	Preston flexible	Siemens 2 × 35hp	Siemens
25-32	Enclosed	1921	Brush	30/42?	Brush Burnley bogies	MV 307 or MV 323 (d)	MV T1 (d)

Livery: Maroon and cream.

Notes
(a) Cars 9 and 12 were fully enclosed about 1926.
(b) The Raworth regenerative controllers were replaced by normal Westinghouse T1/S type between 1912 and 1915.
(c) 30 seats in the saloon, plus two more on each platform, probably only for use at the rear end.
(d) Westinghouse equipment supplied by Metropolitan-Vickers.

Several top covers were resold in 1932 to Darwen Corporation by A. Devey & Co Ltd, dealers.

Key to abbreviations and Manufacturers

Allen West	—	Allen West & Co Ltd, Brighton
Ashbury	—	The Ashbury Railway Carriage & Iron Company, Manchester
BCT	—	Blackpool Corporation Tramways
BEC	—	The British Electric Car Company Ltd, Trafford Park, Manchester
BET	—	The British Electric Traction Company Ltd
Brill	—	The J. G. Brill Company, Philadelphia, USA
BTH	—	The British Thomson-Houston Company Ltd, Rugby
Brush	—	The Brush Electrical Engineering Co Ltd, Loughborough
CP	—	Crompton Parkinson & Co Ltd, Traction Division, Chelmsford
DK	—	Dick, Kerr & Co Ltd, Preston
DCT	—	Darwen Corporation Tramways
ECC	—	The Electric Construction Company Ltd, Wolverhampton
EE	—	The English Electric Co Ltd, Preston
EMB	—	The Electro-Mechanical Brake Co Ltd, West Bromwich
ER&TCW	—	The Electric Railway & Tramway Carriage Works Ltd, Preston
Falcon	—	Falcon Engine & Car Works, Loughborough (owned by Brush)
GE	—	The General Electric Company, Schenectady, USA
GEC	—	General Electric Co Ltd, Witton Works, Birmingham
Hurst Nelson	—	Hurst Nelson & Co Ltd, Motherwell, Scotland
Kitson	—	Kitson & Co Ltd, Airedale Foundry, Leeds
Lancaster	—	The Lancaster Railway Carriage & Wagon Co Ltd
McGuire	—	The McGuire Manufacturing Co Ltd, Bury, Lancashire
MCW	—	Metropolitan-Cammell-Weymann Ltd
Midland	—	Midland Railway-Carriage & Wagon Co Ltd
Milnes	—	Geo. F. Milnes & Co Ltd, Hadley, Shropshire (formerly of Birkenhead)
Milnes Voss	—	G. C. Milnes, Voss & Co Ltd, Birkenhead
M & G	—	Mountain & Gibson Ltd, Bury, Lancashire
M & T	—	Maley & Taunton Ltd, Wednesbury, Staffs
MSCC	—	The Malleable Steel Castings Co (1909) Ltd, Pendleton, Manchester
MV	—	The Metropolitan Vickers Electrical Co Ltd, Trafford Park, Manchester
Peckham	—	Trucks built by or for the Peckham Truck & Engineering Co Ltd. Most post-1908 Peckham trucks were made by the Brush Electrical Engineering Co Ltd
Raworth	—	Raworth's Traction Patents Ltd
Roberts	—	Charles Roberts & Co Ltd, Horbury Junction, near Wakefield
Siemens	—	Siemens Brothers Dynamo Works Ltd, Stafford
Starbuck	—	Starbuck Car & Wagon Co Ltd, Birkenhead
Thomas Green	—	Thomas Green and Son Ltd, Leeds
UEC	—	United Electric Car Company Ltd, Preston
Westinghouse	—	Westinghouse Electric Co Ltd, Trafford Park, Manchester

The Electric Railway & Tramway Carriage Works Ltd (renamed United Electric Car Company Ltd from 25 September 1905) was a subsidiary of Dick, Kerr & Co Ltd, which merged with other electrical companies on 14 December 1918 to form The English Electric Company Ltd.

Bibliography and Acknowledgments

The text of this book is based on Chapter Three of *Great British Tramway Networks* by W. H. Bett and J. C. Gillham, published by the Light Railway Transport League, which itself was based on an article by Mr Bett in *The Modern Tramway* for June 1938. The main book is out of print, but the respective chapters are being republished in the form of illustrated histories of which this is the sixth.

The tramcar fleet lists on pages 51-64 have been compiled by J. H. Price, with the valued assistance of L. P. Calvey, R. Elliott, J. C. Gillham, F. P. Groves, C. C. Hall, M. Harrison, and R. Meadowcroft. The introductory map and the maps of Accrington, Blackburn, Blackpool, Burnley, Lancaster and Lytham were drawn by J. C. Gillham, and the other maps were drawn for this book by Brian Connelly, incorporating information supplied by E. Beddard, J. C. Gillham, R. Meadowcroft, and checked with earlier maps in certain books and articles listed in the bibliography. In certain cases, full information required for the fleet lists could not be traced, or previously-published differences resolved, and the publishers will be pleased to hear from readers who may be able to assist in completing the lists for inclusion in any further edition.

The illustrations have been newly selected for this book, and include several that have not been published before. We are grateful to all the photographers and copyright holders for permission to reproduce them, and to G. E. Baddeley, R. Brook, C. S. Dunbar, G. L. Gundry, J. S. King, M. Harrison and D. Tudor for their help in locating suitable prints. Photographs marked TMS are reproduced by permission of the Tramway Museum Society, from the R. B. Parr collection, and those taken by the late Dr H. A. Whitcombe are reproduced by courtesy of the Science Museum, South Kensington.

Previously published references to which we have referred in compiling this book are listed below and on the following pages.

General

Great British Tramway Networks, by W. H. Bett and J. C. Gillham (Light Railway Transport League, fourth edition, 1962). The present book is based on Chapter Three of this work.

History of the Steam Tram, by Dr H. A. Whitcombe (edited by Charles E. Lee). Oakwood Press, 1954 (reprinted 1961).

Accrington and Rawtenstall

The Tramways of Accrington, 1886-1932. by R. W. Rush. (Light Railway Transport League, 1961). (Also contains notes on Rawtenstall, Blackburn and Darwen).

British Electric Tramcar Design, by R. W. Rush (Oxford Publishing Co, 1976).

The Accrington Corporation Tramways, by R. W. Rush (in *The Modern Tramway,* August 1943, with further notes in October).

Borough of Accrington Transport Department jubilee brochure, 1957.

Hyndburn & Rossendale, 75 Years of Municipal Operation 1907-1982, by Peter Deegan (Omnibus Society, 1982).

Barrow-in-Furness

Barrow-in-Furness Transport, by Ian L. Cormack, M.A. (Author, 1977).

Raworth's Regenerative Demi-Cars, by I. A. Yearsley (in *Tramway Review,* Nos. 76 to 78, 1974).

Seventy-Five Years on Wheels, by Ian L. Cormack, M.A. (Scottish Tramway Museum Society, 1960).

Blackburn and Darwen

The Blackburn and Darwen Tramways, by N. N. Forbes (in *The Modern Tramway,* October to December 1942).

Meeting Blackburn's Trams, by I. A. Yearsley (in *Modern Tramway,* September 1966).

My Fifty Years in Transport, by A. G. Grundy, M.Inst.T. (reprinted from *Transport World,* 1944).

Local Passenger Service in Darwen (in *Modern Transport,* 21 December 1946, 18 January 1947 and 15 February 1947).

Farewell to Blackburn's Trams (BCT souvenir brochure, September 1949).

The First in the Kingdom, by R. P. Fergusson, G. Holden and C. Reilly (Darwen Transport Group, 1981).

Blackpool and Fleetwood Tramroad

Blackpool to Fleetwood, by Brian Turner (Light Railway Transport League, 1977; reprinted from *Modern Tramway*).

North Station to Fleetwood, by G. S. Palmer (Author, 1963).

Diamond Jubilee of the Blackpool & Fleetwood Tramroad, by D. F. Phillips (in *The Tramway Review* No. 25, 1958).

Blackpool Corporation Tramways

The Conduit Tramways of Blackpool, 1885-1899, by D. F. Phillips (in *The Tramway Review* No. 21, 1956).

A Note on the Blackpool Conduit Cars, by D. A. Dougill (in *Tramway Review* No. 54, 1968).

Blackpool Corporation Tramways, 1899-1919, by D. F. Phillips (in *The Tramway Review* No. 28, 1960).

By Tram to the Tower, by G. S. Palmer (Author, 1965).

Blackpool by Tram, by G. S. Palmer and B. R. Turner (Authors, 1968; second revised edition, 1978).

A History of the Blackpool Tramways, by J. R. Henson (in *The Modern Tramway,* April 1949).

The Marton Experiment, by F. K. Pearson, AMIMI (in *Modern Tramway* January and February 1963).

Fleet lists in *Modern Tramway,* November 1961 and July 1968.